What Hawaii LIKES TO EAT™

HANA HOU!

Honolulu **Star★Bulletin** **MidWeek**

Cookbooks By Muriel Miura

As Author

Cook Japanese Hawaiian Style, 1974 (BEST-SELLER 1974)

Hawaiian Pupu Party Planner, 1974

Hawaiian Potpourri, 1975

Maxi Meals for Mini Money, 1975

Cook Japanese Hawaiian Style Volume II, 1976

New World of Cooking with Muriel, 1979

Cooking with Hari and Muriel, 1994

From Hawai'i's Kitchen: Homemade Gifts of Sweets & Treats (Mutual Publishing), 2005
(KA PALAPALA PO'OKELA AWARD—EXCELLENCE IN COOKBOOKS 2006)

Holiday Gift Giving Recipes (Mutual Publishing), 2005

Japanese Cooking—Hawai'i Style (Mutual Publishing), 2006 (BEST-SELLER 2006)

Cookies from Hawai'i's Kitchen (Mutual Publishing), 2006

Hawai'i Cooks with Taro (Mutual Publishing); co-author, 2006

Tastes and Flavors of Hawai'i (Mutual Publishing), 2006

Tastes and Flavors of Pineapple (Mutual Publishing), 2007

What Hawai'i Likes to Eat™ (Mutual Publishing); co-author, 2007
(BEST-SELLER 2007; KA PALAPALA PO'OKELA AWARD—EXCELLENCE IN COOKBOOKS 2008)

Hawai'i's Party Food (Mutual Publishing), 2007

Little Hawaiian Party Food (Mutual Publishing), 2007

Hawai'i's Cooks with SPAM® (Mutual Publishing), 2008

Hawai'i Cooks and Saves (Mutual Publishing), 2008

As Editor/Chair

Heritage of Hawai'i Cookbook Volume I (Gasco), 1965

Heritage of Hawai'i Cookbook Volume II (Gasco), 1970

The Legacy of the Japanese in Hawai'i: Cuisine (JCCH), 1989

Tastes & Tales of Mō'ili'ili (Mō'ili'ili Community Center), 1997

A Tradition of Aloha Cookbook (Japanese Women's Society), 1998

Flavors of Aloha (Japanese Women's Society), 2001

What Hawai'i LIKES TO EAT™

HANA HOU!

Muriel Miura

with

Galyn "Gay" Wong

Mutual Publishing

What Hawai'i LIKES TO EAT™

HANA HOU!

Muriel Miura

with

Galyn "Gay" Wong

&

special guest
Chef Martin Wyss

Food photography by Kaz Tanabe

Mutual Publishing

ISBN-10: 1-56647-906-1
ISBN-13: 978-1-56647-906-6

Library of Congress Cataloging-in-Publication Data

Miura, Muriel.
   What Hawai'i likes to eat-- hana hou / Muriel Miura with Galyn
   "Gay" Wong ; food photography by Kaz Tanabe.
      p. cm.
   Includes index.
   ISBN 1-56647-906-1 (hardcover : alk. paper)
   1. Hawaiian cookery. I. Wong, Galyn. II. Title.
   TX724.5.H3M5923 2009
   641.5969--dc22

                        2009022835

Food photography by Kaz Tanabe, unless otherwise noted
Spot photography from dreamstime.com:
   p. 4 © Chode; p. 6 © Maja Schon; p. 10 © Andreea Dobrescu;
   p. 51 © Chiyacat; p. 67 © Tomboy2290; p. 73 © Andrzej
   Tokarski; p. 93 © Andrey Butenko; p. 96 © Alvin Teo; p. 97
   © Kiankhoon; p. 99 © Ivan Mikhaylov; p. 101 © Shariff
   Che'Lah; p. 107 © Lijuan Guo; p. 110 © Dušan Zidar;
   p. 112 © Ruben Paz; p. 116 © Wikki; Casaalmare; p. 118
   © Mchudo; p. 124 © Janet Hastings; p. 130 © Mailthepic;
   p. 137 © Antonio Muñoz Palomares, Norman Chan; p. 138
   © Paul Cowan; p. 146 © Viktorfischer; p. 153 © Maram; p. 155
   © Lukasz Olek; p. 157 © Branislav Senic; p. 164 © Nataliya
   Evmenenko; p. 167 © Christy Thompson; p. 181 © Johnny Lye;
   p. 190 © Homestudiofoto; p. 191 © Nadia Zagainova

Food photography art direction by Jane Gillespie
Food styling by Hideaki "Santa" Miyoshi and Gay Wong
Flowers by Rainforest
Design by Nancy Watanabe, Leo Gonzalez, and Courtney
   Young
Cover design by Leo Gonzalez

First Printing, September 2009

Mutual Publishing, LLC
1215 Center Street, Suite 210
Honolulu, Hawai'i 96816
Ph: 808-732-1709 / Fax: 808-734-4094
email: info@mutualpublishing.com
www.mutualpublishing.com

Printed in China

Dedication

*To all food lovers who enjoy
the unique flavors of our Hawai'i.*

Contents

Mr. Kamada's first refrigerated truck, circa 1930 (Muriel Miura)

Remembering...

Omiyage...
the Custom of Gift-Giving

Simply Sushi

E Pā'ina Kākou...
Let's Party!

WOW...
a Treasury of Desserts

Appendices

Acknowledgments

*M*ahalo Nui Loa to all of the chefs, foodie friends, and our loving families who shared their recipes and stories contained in this cookbook. With special thanks to:

Richard Ahn, Ernie Baustista, Billy Browning, Farrant Chung, Rob Domingo, Ian Gillespie, Leo Gonzalez, Sandie Hata, Kyle Higa, Jennie In, Leigh Ito, James Kau, Duane Kawamoto, Kari Kimura, Kelli Kimura, Kristi Kimura, Joe Kimura, Herbert & Harue Lee, Jeffery Lee, Tim Masten, Michael Miyashiro, Linda & Natasha Miller, Alfred Monaco, Malia & Jade Ogoshi, Tami & Raymond Orozco, Mili Pang, Tylun Pang, Terry Phillips, Kelvin Ro, Erika Roberts, Tracey Russell, Larry Shigaki, Betty Shimabukuro, Lynette Shimabukuro, Goran Streng, Russell Siu, Mona Taga, Audrey Tam, Alan Wong, Thomas & Setsuko Wong, Jan Woodring, Martin & Jeanie Wyss, Pat Yamamoto, Fern Yamane, Mahealani Youn, Courtney Young, and Terrance Young.

(Mutual Publishing)

Thanks also to you, the reader, for embracing the first volume of *What Hawai'i Likes to Eat*™ and making this sequel possible.

Foreword

I have to admit, at first I didn't see the point. Why another collection of local-style recipes, another journey through Hawai'i's melting-pot, and plantation heritage? Why another cookbook of island favorites?

That cookbook was *What Hawai'i Likes to Eat*™, which I wrote in 2006 with Muriel Miura, based on a concept originated by our publisher, Bennett Hymer. I took on the project for the chance to work with Muriel, whom I consider the grand dame of local recipe lore and one of the savviest people around. But I still wondered who was going to care.

Well, they were right and I was wrong. Response to the book was far beyond my expectations. *What Hawai'i Likes to Eat*™ was good-looking and tasty-sounding. People responded to our themes and our search through Hawai'i's culinary past. And they weren't just being nice to me, they were putting up real American dollars for their copies, as well as gift copies for aunties, grandpas and various cousins tucked away in Mainland cities far from chicken katsu plates and SPAM® musubi.

Within a year, Bennett and Muriel were talking about a second volume. Again, I didn't see the point. I questioned who'd be interested in a similar book so soon. But again, they'll be right and I'll be wrong. More power to them. Food defines us — and not just our sense of place and taste. It links us through time, space and across generations. A book that emphasizes those connections, providing the recipes that sustain our food traditions — well, that's a book that matters.

*Preparing for the imu, circa 1930s
(Hawai'i State Archives)*

I wasn't able to participate in "Hana Hou," due to demands of my day job at the *Honolulu Star-Bulletin*. You'll see by browsing this collection that Muriel didn't need me. This time, her themes reflect a sense of sharing — consider her chapters on omiyage, on food for parties, and "Remembering," a reflection of our shared past when it comes to dining out. Use this book. Don't just admire the pretty pictures or stroll down memory lane by browsing the recipe titles. Cook from it. You'll be better fed, in body and soul.

—BETTY SHIMABUKURO

Preface

Aloha,

Enjoying the myriad of food Hawai'i has to offer means putting the emphasis on good taste, easy preparation and fun. The recipes selected mirror Hawai'i's ethnic diversity and its informal, friendly lifestyle. They range from the quick and easy-to-prepare to a few lavish ones for special occasions. Regardless of the recipe, all directions are simply written and easy-to-follow.

The catalyst for the collection of these recipes and the sequel to *What Hawai'i Likes To Eat™* is you, the reader, and it is based on everyone's common passion for good food. Because we are fortunate to be involved professionally with chefs and foodies, it made it possible for us to compile a great collection of recipes just for you.

There's nothing exotic about our recipe collection…in fact, it's rather plain and simple!

(Hawai'i State Archives)

We bring you many "favorites from the past," plus some new ideas too—all of which are good eating! Many of the recipes are treasured ones, which have stood the test of time, from our foodie friends, families, and chefs. They are the result of our combined experiences gained from working with people in the food industry and from immensely enjoying the fun of cooking over the years.

In working together, sharing ideas, stories and recipes, we've truly discovered the magic of friendship and the joy of sharing.

We hope that you will embrace *What Hawai'i Likes To Eat™…Hana Hou!* and join us in the joy of cooking through the pages of this book. Enjoy the stories we share and use these recipes as a guide to create some of your own. In doing so, you'll discover that there is no limit to food horizons. Enjoy them in good health!

—MURIEL MIURA & GALYN WONG

Introduction

*H*awai'i, the island state, is often referred to as "The Paradise of the Pacific" and still evokes images of exotic beauty and escape. Many leave our islands with memories of the hospitable people, beautiful scenery and exotic foods. As a result, people are always asking about what Hawai'i likes to eat.

Soda fountain in Benson Smith Drug Store, Fort Street, circa 1937 (Bishop Museum)

Hawai'i's beauty, its tropical climate and its population of immigrants from all parts of the world have fostered a lifestyle that is fresh, healthy and hearty. Hawai'i's people love the outdoors, casual cooking and entertain with diverse culinary delights. A gathering in Hawai'i often has dishes representing the ethnicity of the people who call Hawai'i home, from Kālua Pig to Strawberry Mousse.

Many recipes are old-time favorites, handed down through generations, while others are more contemporary and come from chefs and our foodie friends. However, each has been edited for clarity, editorial uniformity and ease of preparation to fit today's busy lifestyle, standing the test of time.

One may say that our taste is eclectic with the flavors of many lands influencing our cuisine. Dishes such as saimin or poke wraps are popular only in Hawai'i and where else but in Hawai'i would you order Portuguese Sausage and eggs for breakfast? An omiyage of cookies or chutney is a must when you're visiting someone off island…it is the custom. Or where else but in Hawai'i is there a Chinese restaurant that serves curried lobster with fried haupia? If you have a craving for rice, then it's a stop at the nearest sushi bar where you can order a variety of nigiri sushi topped with fresh 'ahi, aku or even 'ōpakapaka. As for desserts, Hawai'i's people love their sweets of bread puddings to lava cake and more. When it's party time you'll see everything from gon lo mein to exotic green tea noodle shrimp tempura.

This is only a glance at how many exciting recipes there are in this cookbook along with lovely photos and quaint stories of some of the dishes…all are recipes and ideas that will help any novice cook like a chef. As you browse through the recipes of this book, you'll find a reflection of the rich and colorful heritage of Hawai'i.

Only in Hawai'i

*O*nce again, we dedicate this chapter to audacity—our willingness to take bold risks in food combinations and our nerve, sometimes defiant, to take a variety of ethnic foods and make them our own. Our culinary history is one of acceptance and assimilation—it's flavorful, enticing, and inspired by the people who have made these islands their home. The recipes collected here reflect Hawai'i's rich diversity and cultural heritage.

Local favorites, such as Portuguese Sweet Bread and Saimin, sit alongside new creations from some of Hawai'i's celebrity chefs, such as Kālua Pig BLT Sandwich. These recipes display our willingness to recreate and redefine ourselves while being mindful of the past and how it relates to our present and our future. Throughout, an attempt has been made to capture the essence of aloha in every dish.

Kau kau time for the plantation workers in the sugar cane field, circa 1900s (Bishop Museum)

'Ahi/Aku Poke Wraps

raditional Hawaiian poke, which means to cut or slice, was prepared with cubed fish flesh which was then flavored with ingredients available in ancient times—sea salt, 'inamona, (roasted, ground kukui nuts). Contemporary poke combines ancient preparation with flavors from the various cultures that have come to Hawai'i since ancient times. It is not uncommon to find wasabi, soy sauce, or won tons in a modern poke dish.

YIELD: 12 ROLLS

6 sheets bahn trang (dried rice paper wrappers)

FILLING:

1 pound 'ahi or aku, cut in ½-inch cubes
½ cup limu kohu (seaweed), blanched and chopped
¼ cup minced green onion
¼ cup Maui onion, thinly sliced
¼ teaspoon sesame oil
2 teaspoons soy sauce
1 teaspoon Hawaiian salt
Hot chili sauce to taste

WASABI DIPPING SAUCE:

1 tablespoon wasabi powder
1 tablespoon water
¼ cup soy sauce
½ teaspoon dashi-no-moto
3 tablespoons hot water

TO MAKE FILLING: Combine all ingredients in medium bowl; toss lightly to mix well. Refrigerate 1 hour before serving.

TO MAKE WASABI DIPPING SAUCE: Stir together wasabi powder with water; add soy sauce, dashi-no-moto and hot water. Mix well; set aside.

TO MAKE POKE WRAP: Dip each bahn trang in a bowl of warm water for a few seconds to soften. Remove; dry with paper towel. Place about 2 to 3 tablespoons of Filling on lower one-third of bahn trang; fold bottom of the wrapper over the Filling. Fold the left and right edges over toward center and roll up tightly into a cylinder, pressing to seal. Repeat until wrappers are all used. Slice each roll in half and serve chilled with Wasabi Dipping Sauce.

VARIATIONS:
- Fill bahn trang with shrimp, clams, lobster, an assortment of seafoods instead of fish.
- Combine sushi rice with vegetables and seafood of choice.
- Combine steamed rice with teriyaki meat and vegetables of choice.

NOTE: Bahn trang (dried rice paper wrappers) are sold in Asian stores or in the oriental/Asian food section of supermarkets in plastic packets containing about 10 or more wrappers, which are about 8 to 10 inches in diameter.

Easy Boiled Peanuts

ack in the good ol' days, football and baseball games were played Honolulu Stadium, located at the corner of Isenberg and South King Streets. Back then, spectators didn't have the variety of concession choices offered at modern stadiums. Still there was good eating to be had. There were the usual snacks—popcorn, soda, ice cream, chips, shaved ice, ca bars, hot dogs, and hamburgers—but, before entering the stadium, nearly everyone stopped to buy boiled peanuts from the "Peanut Lady," who sold them in brown paper bags outside the main gate.

YIELD: 2 POUNDS

2 pounds raw peanuts in shell
½ cup Hawaiian salt
2 to 3 whole star anise
1 tablespoon sugar

Place peanuts in a large pot and cover with water. Add salt, star anise and sugar. Bring to a boil, cover, and simmer for 1 to 1½ hours, stirring occasionally, or until peanuts are tender but firm. Add more water as necessary to keep peanuts covered with water. Adjust seasoning as necessary. Cool and drain. Will keep in refrigerator 2 to 3 days.

(Ian Gillespie)

4

Portuguese Sweet Bread
(Pao Doce)

Pao Doce, a traditional Portuguese bread usually baked at Christmas and Easter, can be found year-round in Hawai'i. This sweet bread has become a local favorite used to make sandwiches, bread puddings, or simply sliced and served.

Sprinkle yeast over potato water. Stir in ¼ cup of sugar, potatoes and ginger; cover and let rise until doubled. Add salt to scalded milk; cook to lukewarm. In a small mixing bowl, gradually beat in remaining sugar; stir into yeast mixture. Add butter and mix well. Stir in 2 cups of flour, then milk. Add 2 more cups of flour; beat for 5 minutes. Stir in enough of remaining flour to make a stiff dough.

Place on a lightly floured board and knead in remaining flour until dough is smooth and elastic, about 8 to 10 minutes. Place dough in a large greased bowl, turning once to grease top. Cover; let rise until doubled. Grease four 9 x 5 x 3-inch loaf pans. Divide dough into fourths on a lightly floured board. Shape each fourth into a loaf; place in prepared pans. Cover; let rise until doubled. Brush loaves with beaten egg. Bake at 325°F for 45 to 50 minutes or until brown.

Making bread the Portuguese way, circa 1920s (Bishop Museum)

YIELD: 4 LOAVES

2 packages active dry yeast
½ cup warm potato water
¼ cup sugar
1 cup mashed potatoes
⅛ teaspoon ginger, optional
1½ teaspoons salt
½ cup milk, scalded
1¾ cups sugar
½ cup butter or margarine, melted
8 to 10 cups flour
6 eggs, beaten

Sweet Bread French Toast
Tangö Contemporary Café

The sweet flavor of Pao Doce or Portuguese sweet bread makes it a favorite of breakfasts and brunches. When Goran Streng, co-owner and executive chef of Tangö Contemporary Café, prepares his French toast using sweet bread saturated with a custard-like dip of eggs and milk, the resulting dish is transformed into something like a rich bread pudding. Delicious!

YIELD: ABOUT 8 SERVINGS

8 whole eggs
4 egg yolks
1 quart milk
2 tablespoons vanilla extract
2 tablespoons ground cinnamon
1 cup sugar
1 loaf (1 lb.) Portuguese sweetbread

Beat eggs, egg yolks, milk, vanilla extract, ground cinnamon and sugar together in a medium size mixing bowl. Slice sweet bread into ½-inch thick slices; dip them into the egg mixture and gently turn them until they are saturated on both sides.

Heat a lightly greased or nonstick griddle or pan over medium heat. Lift the slices from the egg mixture, let excess liquid drip off, and place them on the griddle, in batches if necessary; cook until golden brown, about 3 minutes per side. Keep warm. Serve with fresh berries and maple syrup.

Mui *(Chinese Preserves)*

Honolulu Chinatown crack seed shop, circa 1971
(Hawaiʻi State Archives)

Making mui (preserves) most likely became popular in Hawaiʻi during the Second World War as a means of preserving fruits in short supply due to rationing. During my childhood in the 1940s, I can remember seeing covered jars of fruits being "aged" on kitchen counters at homes of friends. On occasion, one of my aunts made some yummy prune mui for our family.

The Chinese preserved fruit, mui, is usually plums. Creative cooks, however, also make mui using other fruits. In addition to traditional mui, we've included other preserves influenced by the Chinese preserving process in this section.

Apricot Mui

YIELD: ABOUT 2 PINTS

1 cup brown sugar, packed
1 cup water
1 tablespoon molasses
¼ teaspoon Chinese five-spices
2 tablespoons rock salt
1 teaspoon lemon juice
4 packages (8 oz. each) dried apricots
   (peaches or prunes)

Combine all ingredients, except apricots, in large saucepan; bring to a boil and add apricots; cook 1 minute. Remove from heat and let cool. Pack into sterilized jar and refrigerate.

Fruit Preserves

YIELD: VARIES

1 box dried fruit (prunes, apricots,
   peaches or combination as desired)
¼ cup sugar
¼ cup salt
Juice of 2 large lemons

Combine all ingredients in large jar; cover and shake well to coat fruits with sugar-lemon mixture. Leave in the sun at least three to four days before serving.

Mango Seed

Peel green mangoes. Cut in half, through the seed, if possible. Remove meat in seed and sprinkle salt over mangoes. Dry in single layers in the sun for four days.

Place dried mangoes in large pot and add water to cover; cook 30 minutes. Drain. Add sugar and molasses; cover and cook over low heat for 15 minutes. Add spices and coloring. Cool for 5 minutes. Store in sterilized jars.

YIELD: ABOUT 1½ QUARTS

35 green mangoes
Hawaiian salt
Water
3 cups brown sugar, packed
¼ cup dark molasses
½ teaspoon Chinese five-spices
½ teaspoon red food coloring

Star Fruit Seed

Rinse dried star fruit and cook it with all the ingredients until shiny and transparent in appearance. Store in sterilized jars and let stand 2 to 3 days before serving.

NOTE: 1 quart prunes may be substituted for 1 quart dried star fruit.

YIELD: ABOUT 1 QUART

1 quart dried star fruit, slice
lengthwise or crosswise
to shape like a star; dry for
not more than 1½ days
3 lemons
1½ tablespoons salt
6 tablespoons sugar
⅛ teaspoon cloves, allspice or
Chinese five-spices
2½ tablespoons vinegar

4 pounds dried prunes
2 cups lemon juice
1 cup sugar
½ cup sugar
½ teaspoon powdered cloves
1 teaspoon lemon zest

1 box (1 lb.) light brown sugar
3 tablespoons Hawaiian salt
3 tablespoons scotch, bourbon, brandy or sherry
1 teaspoon Chinese five-spices
10 whole cloves
1½ cups (about 7 lemons) fresh lemon juice
8 packages (12 oz. each) pitted prunes
1 large package (6-8oz.) preserved lemon peel, cut into pieces
1 large package (4 oz.) seedless li hing mui

Salty Preserved Prunes

Combine all ingredients in large pot and cook for 10 minutes or leave in a jar outdoors in the sun for at least two weeks, shaking it occasionally to distribute the flavor.

Prune Mui

Combine brown sugar, salt, whiskey, Chinese five-spices, cloves and lemon juice in a large container with cover. Add and toss prunes, lemon peel and li hing mui. Cover and let stand for four days or longer. Toss/mix at least two times daily.

Kālua Pig BLT Sandwich
The Pineapple Room ~ *Macy's Ala Moana*

Kālua pig is a local favorite. The dish is traditionally prepared in an imu, or underground oven. The pig can take hours to cook. When the pork is at last fully cooked it is raised from the imu to take its place as the delicious centerpiece of any Hawaiian lū'au or local gathering.

Chef Alan Wong has put his own spin on this local classic. Served on an onion bun with Caesar Salad, the Kālua Pig BLT has become one of the most popular dishes at Alan Wong's Pineapple Room located on the top floor of Macy's Ala Moana. It is truly an awesome sandwich and one that you'll just have to try!

YIELD: 4 SERVINGS

¾ pound oven kālua pig
1 large tomato, cut 4 thin slices
2 tablespoons minced onion
1 tablespoon minced green onion
2 tablespoons Boursin cheese
¼ cup mayonnaise
4 onion buns, split
4 slices cooked thick bacon, cut into thirds
4 leaves lettuce, washed and dried (optional)

Heat kālua pig in small skillet only until heated through; set aside. Save 4 slices tomato on the side; mince remaining tomato and combine with minced onion and green onion in small bowl; mix well. In small dish, mix together Boursin cheese and mayonnaise; spread tops and bottoms of buns with mixture. Place about 3 ounces kālua pig on each bottom half of buns then top with minced tomato-onion mixture, bacon, slice of tomato and lettuce if used. Top with remaining half of bun.

The traditional kālua pig is a whole pig prepared in an underground oven, or imu. It takes hours to cook the pork and when it is done to perfection, it is raised from the imu in the midst of a ceremony of prayer, music and dancing at a Hawaiian lū'au. Today, kālua pig, a Hawaiian favorite is often prepared in the kitchen using pork butt or shoulder.

If kālua pig in not available, oven-smoke and braise pork roast in a shallow pan by combining 1½ teaspoons liquid smoke with about 3 cups of chicken broth and placing the pork roast in the broth to cook for 3 to 3½ hours or until fork-tender. Shred cooked pork using two forks and keep in the broth until ready to use. Freeze unused smoked pork for later use.

VARIATIONS: Smoked pork, chicken, turkey or duck may be substituted for kālua pig.

Portuguese Sausage *(Linguica)*

In Hawai'i, a typical breakfast will more than likely contain Portuguese sausage and eggs served with two scoops of rice. Portuguese sausage, a spicy variety of pork sausage, is a local comfort food and is used in a number of popular island dishes such as Portuguese bean soup and fried rice.

(Ian Gillespie)

YIELD: ABOUT 2½ POUNDS

½ cup water

¼ teaspoon red food coloring, optional

2 pounds pork, coarsely ground or chopped

1 tablespoon vinegar

4 cloves garlic, minced

⅛ teaspoon cumin, optional

2½ teaspoons salt or 1½ teaspoons Hawaiian salt

½ teaspoon cayenne pepper

¼ teaspoon paprika

2 chili peppers, chopped

¼ teaspoons liquid smoke

OPTIONAL:

½ pound sausage casings (chitterlings or small pork intestines), thoroughly cleaned

Combine water and food coloring. Mix with remaining ingredients except sausage casings. Cover and refrigerate for 2 days, stirring occasionally. Shape into thin patties and pan-fry in nonstick skillet for 5 to 10 minutes or until cooked through.

If desired, raw pork filling may be stuffed into thoroughly cleaned casings. Tie one end of each length of casing; press out all air through the other end and fill casing with pork mixture by using a funnel or cake decorator without the tube attached. Pack tightly. Tie with string at desired intervals to form links. Place links in ¼-cup water in skillet; cover and simmer 35 minutes. Drain and continue cooking, uncovered, over low heat until well-browned and cooked through. If smoker is available, sausage may be smoked for 6 to 7 hours.

TIPS:
- To clean sausage casings cut into 15 to 20-inch lengths. Scrub inside and outside of casings at least 5 times with rock salt and flour, rinsing well each time. Wash well in vinegar solution; rinse well.
- Another method of cleaning casings is to soak them in warm water for 3 to 4 hours, then rinse with running water by placing one end over the end of a faucet and allowing the water to run through. Pour vinegar through and rinse multiple times.

Oriental Popcorn

Pour butter over popcorn in large bowl; sprinkle furikake and toss to distribute evenly. Add nuts and arare; toss again. Best if eaten immediately or may be stored in airtight container.

VARIATIONS:

- Substitute honey glazed macadamia nuts for unsalted macadamia nuts.
- Sprinkle with 3 tablespoons li hing powder; omit nori furikake.
- Substitute shiso furikake for nori furikake.

YIELD: ABOUT 8 CUPS

8 cups air-popped popcorn
⅓ cup melted butter or margarine
½ cup nori furikake
½ cup unsalted macadamia nut halves
1 cup arare (Japanese rice crackers)

Red Coconut Candy

As a youngster I remember these red coconut balls as being one of our favorite "candies." It was a very tasty snack or dessert which was easy to make and was also sold at the little "mom and pop" stores in our neighborhood.

Mix coconut and corn syrup together thoroughly. Roll into 1-inch balls. Combine sugar and food coloring; mix well. Roll coconut balls in colored sugar and chill at least an hour in the refrigerator before serving.

YIELD: ABOUT 30 BALLS

1 package (7 oz.) sweetened flaked coconut
½ cup corn syrup
¼ cup sugar
¼ teaspoon red food coloring or coloring of choice

Mauna Kea Street, Chinatown, circa 1978 (Bishop Museum)

Saimin

Saimin immigrated to Hawai'i with the Japanese. These thin wheat noodles where commonly sold by street vendors, who served their simple fare in a steaming garnished with char siu, strips of luncheon meat, green onion and fried egg.

Since then, saimin has become a favorite comfort food in the Islands. No one knows this better than, Hawai'i Restaurant Hall of Fame honoree, Shiro "Mistah Saimin" Matsuo. Shiro's saimin teems with garnishes like roast beef, imitation crab, eggrolls, shrimp tempura, Chinese-style roast pork, fish cake, won tons, and assorted vegetables, transforming this former snack into a hearty meal.

Cold Saimin Salad
(Hiya Ramen)

Chilled saimin, topped with condiments and laced with a zesty ponzu sauce, this is a recipe my father shared with me nearly four decades ago. This dish is a refreshing variation on traditional saimin and perfectly suited for Hawai'i's tropical climate.

Cook saimin as directed on package. Rinse, drain well and chill. Arrange noodles in individual serving bowls (on ice, if desired); arrange condiments attractively over noodles.

TO PREPARE SAUCE: Combine all ingredients in a jar with cover; cover and shake vigorously until well combined. Pour over arrangement of condiments and noodles just before serving.

YIELD: ABOUT 4 SERVINGS

1 package (12 oz.) dried or raw saimin

CONDIMENTS:

1 small cucumber, slivered
2 cups bean sprouts, blanched
1 cup minced green onion
1 cup luncheon meat, slivered
1 tablespoon toasted sesame seeds
Fried egg strips

SAUCE:

½ cup rice vinegar
½ cup soy sauce
½ cup sugar
¼ teaspoon sesame seed oil
1 package dashi-no-moto
Few drops hot sauce, optional

GARNISH:

Minced green onion
Nori slivers

Fried Saimin *(Yaki Ramen)*

This fast and simple dish is perfect for those times when unexpected company drops by or when the kids need a quick snack.

YIELD: 4-6 SERVINGS

½ cup chicken or pork, slivered
1 tablespoon salad oil
6 shrimp, cleaned and minced
⅓ cup bamboo shoots, sliced
½ cup celery, sliced diagonally
½ cup green onion, cut in
    1-inch lengths
½ pound bean sprouts,
    washed and drained
1 tablespoon toasted sesame
    seeds
1 pound fresh cooked ramen

SEASONINGS:

2 teaspoons soy sauce
¼ cup chicken broth
1 teaspoon salt

GARNISHES:

2 tablespoons toasted sesame
    seeds
¼ cup minced green onion
Chinese parsley sprigs

(Ian Gillespie)

Stir-fry chicken or pork in hot oil for 2 minutes. Add shrimp, stir-fry additional minute. Add vegetables, noodles and seasonings; stir-fry 1 minute to heat through. Garnish with sesame seeds, green onions and Chinese parsley.

VARIATIONS: Cooked soba, udon or chuka soba (chow mein) may be substituted for ramen.

SPAM® Temaki Sushi

Hawai'i loves to eat SPAM®! Folks here consume more than more than six million cans of SPAM® per year, or six cans per person per year—the most in the United States. People in Hawai'i are passionate about this canned luncheon meat, creatively combining it with just about anything—as the following recipes demonstrate.

Place a sheet of sushi nori in palm of hand and spoon about ¼ cup Sushi Rice over and spread evenly on nori. Place a streak of wasabi paste along center of rice and lay strips of SPAM®, cucumber and radish sprouts. Wrap nori around filling, starting at lower end of nori and rolling diagonally into cone shape. Serve with soy sauce, if desired.

YIELD: 10 ROLLS

5 sheets sushi nori, cut in half
2½ cups Sushi Rice
   (see page 94)
Wasabi paste
10 pieces SPAM® strips or logs
10 cucumber strips, cut into
   5-inch lengths
Radish sprouts
Soy sauce

Teriyaki Meat On-A-Stick

Teriyaki Meat on-a-stick is a traditional side dish for saimin. I can remember during small-kid-time always being served a bowl of hot saimin with Teriyaki Meat on-a-stick for weekend lunches or as a snack.

Cut meat into strips about ¼-inch thick; cut strips into 1½-inch pieces. Thread 4 or 5 pieces on bamboo sticks or small skewers. Marinate for 30 minutes in teriyaki sauce and broil. Serve with hot bowl of saimin noodles in broth. Cubes of uncooked chicken may be substituted for beef.

YIELD: ABOUT 40 STICKS

½ cup teriyaki sauce
  (recipe below)
3 pounds round steak, 1-inch
  thick

Teriyaki Sauce

Soy sauce-based marinades give any meat a salty, yet tangy flavor perfect for any mixed plate. For a touch of Korean flavor, add sesame oil, toasted sesame seeds, hot sauce and minced green onion to the basic sauce.

Combine all ingredients in jar; cover and refrigerate. Shake well before using as marinade for meats, poultry and seafood.

YIELD: ABOUT 1 QUART

2 cups soy sauce
¼ cup water
2 cups sugar
¼ cup mirin or sherry
1 or 2 cloves garlic, crushed
1 piece, (½-inch) fresh ginger,
  crushed

Kau kau time when food was shared, circa 1900s (Bishop Museum)

Mixed Plate

The mixed plate is a local culinary institution that finds its origins in plantation life. Field hands and workers employed by the sugar and pineapple plantations throughout the Islands brought home lunches to work everyday, often sharing their meals with other workers. Just as the workers represented a wide cross-section of ethnicities and cultures, so to did their meals, which most likely contained char siu from China, teriyaki chicken from Japan, lumpia from the Philippines, kimchee from Korea, and so on.

Nowadays, mixed plate lunches are sold at most delicatessens, or okazu-ya, and local fast food places, as well as at local supermarkets. Plate lunches are almost always comprised of two scoops rice, one scoop macaroni salad with the entrée(s) of choice. The combinations of dishes vary from place to place and customers can make their own entrée choices from beef stew to pork adobo. No matter what combination the customer chooses, however, the result will be filling and tasty!

Macaroni Salad

YIELD: 4-6 SERVINGS

½ cup minced round onion
½ cup minced celery
2 tablespoons sweet pickle relish, optional
¼ cup minced parsley
¼ cup minced kamaboko, optional
6 cups elbow macaroni, well-drained and chilled
2 hard cooked eggs, coarsely chopped
1½ cups mayonnaise
½ teaspoon salt
Fresh ground pepper to taste

In Hawai'i a mixed plate is simply not a mixed plate without a scoop of macaroni salad. There are numerous recipes for this Island favorite, but following is a simple one that my family enjoys. Try it!

Combine onion, celery, pickle relish, parsley, kamaboko, and macaroni. Toss lightly to mix well. Add remaining ingredients; toss. Adjust mayonnaise, salt and pepper to taste. Chill. Serve on bed of greens or place a scoop on plate lunch.

Taro Stew

Often referred to as paniolo (cowboy) stew, the Hawaiian taro is used in this soup in place of potatoes. This stew will serve as a hearty treat to all the rough and tumble cowpokes in your house!

Combine flour, salt and pepper; dredge beef in flour mixture. In a large pot, brown beef in hot oil. Stir in onion, garlic, ginger, red pepper and peppercorns. Add water; bring to a boil and cover; simmer for 1½ to 2 hours or until beef is tender. Add carrots and taro; cover and simmer additional 30 to 40 minutes. Add green onions and salt just before serving. Adjust seasoning as necessary. Thicken stew to desired consistency with poi, if used.

YIELD: 6 SERVINGS

¼ cup flour
¾ teaspoon salt
⅛ teaspoon pepper
2 pounds boneless stewing beef
2 tablespoons canola oil
1 large onion, sliced
1 clove garlic, crushed
1 small piece fresh ginger, crushed
1 Hawaiian red pepper, seeded and minced
½ teaspoon peppercorns
5-6 cups water
2 large carrots, peeled and cut into 1-inch pieces
2 pounds taro, peeled and cut into 1-inch pieces
1 cup chopped green onions
1 teaspoon Hawaiian salt
Poi to thicken, optional

Bento

The bento box was first introduced to Hawai'i by Japanese plantation workers who carried their lunches in a Bento Bako (lunch box). These boxes often contained typical Japanese fare such as musubi, tsukemono (pickled vegetable), fried fish, teriyaki beef, and scrambled shoyu egg. As the Japanese assimilated with people from other lands in Hawai'i, the bento began to be adopted by other cultures. Today bento boxes often include fried lumpia or kimchee.

Tsukemono *(Pickled Vegetable)*

At one time, every bento box contained musubi and probably some type of Tsukemono (pickled vegetable) along with a main okazu (entrée) such as fried fish, teriyaki beef, shoyu chicken, and fried eggs.

SUGGESTED VEGETABLES: Turnips, radishes, head cabbage, cucumbers, eggplants, won bok/napa or Chinese mustard cabbage.

Combine all ingredients listed; mix well and add vegetables of choice in large container. Apply 3 to 5 pound weight on top of vegetables and let stand 1 to 2 days in refrigerator or at room temperature. Rinse and squeeze out excess liquid. Cut into bite-size pieces and serve as side dish with soy sauce.

YIELD: ABOUT 2 CUPS

SOLUTION:

1¾ cups water
1, 5-inch piece dashi kombu
1½ to 3 tablespoons Hawaiian salt
1½ tablespoons sugar
½ teaspoon soy sauce
1½ teaspoons rice vinegar
1½ teaspoons sake (rice wine)

Musubi/Onigiri *(Rice Balls)*

YIELD: ABOUT 8 OR 9 MUSUBI

3 cups short grain rice
3¼ cups water
4 sheets nori (seaweed laver)

SUGGESTED CONDIMENTS:

Smoked salmon
Umeboshi (pickled plum),
    remove seed and mash
Canned tuna, cook in teriyaki
    sauce
Cooked SPAM®, minced
Nori tsukudani (seaweed paste)
Seasoned hijiki (cooked seaweed)
Kālua pig (smoked pork)
Char siu (sweet roasted pork)
Kimchee (Korean-style spicy
    pickled vegetables)
Cooked teriyaki beef, pork or
    chicken, chopped
Toasted sesame seeds
Nori (seaweed laver), cut into
    strips as desired
Aonori (crushed green seaweed)

y "oba-ba" (grandma) made the best musubi. The rice always came out slightly burnt from the old, black Japanese rice pot with its wooden lid, cooked over the open outdoor fire (kamadaki gohan), I loved that part the best, it was crusty and delicious.

Onigiri or musubi, the Japanese name for rice balls, means hand-molded rice. Short-grain rice is ideal for making musubi. In Hawai'i, you'll find musubi filled with a variety of ingredients—salmon, tuna, umeboshi, nori tsukudani, seasoned hijiki or even chopped kālua pig, minced char siu, or kimchee.

Wash rice, drain and place in pot with cover. Add water and let stand 1 hour before cooking. Cover and bring to a boil; reduce heat and simmer over low heat 15 minutes. Turn heat "off" and leave covered for 15 minutes. Stir with wooden spatula and fluff rice; cool for 10 to 15 minutes before making musubi.

TRIANGULAR MUSUBI: Wet hands and sprinkle with salt. Mold handful of rice into triangular shape; make a well in the center; add desired filling and cover filling with one teaspoon rice; press firmly to close. Sprinkle with sesame seeds and put a ¾ to 1-inch band of nori around outer edge of triangle.

OBLONG MUSUBI: Wet hands and sprinkle with salt. Mold handful of rice into rounded oblong shapes. Put a 1-inch band of nori around middle of musubi; sprinkle one end with sesame seeds and the other end with aonri, if desired.

SEASONED MUSUBI: Toss hot, cooked rice with seasoned hijiki, sesame seeds or any type of sauce as desired then shape into triangular, oblong or round musubi; wrap band of nori around outer edge.

Double-Crusted Coconut Pie

Coconut cream pies are the rage today but there was a time when the double crust coconut pie, filled with grated fresh coconut, was popular. While shredded coconut is commonly found at the grocer's today, when I was younger, one had to husk and grate the coconut oneself. While I have always loved the taste of fresh coconut, I very much disliked the arduous process of getting at the sweet flesh, which was left to the boys while I did the baking.

YIELD: 8 SERVINGS

Pastry for 2-crust pie
6 cups shredded coconut
⅔ cup sugar
¼ teaspoon salt
1 cup coconut milk
3 egg whites
Milk

Line 9-inch pie pan with pastry. In medium bowl, combine coconut, sugar, salt and coconut milk. In small mixing bowl, beat egg whites until stiff peaks form. Gently fold meringue into coconut mixture; pour into pastry lined pie pan; cover with top crust and flute edges. Brush crust lightly with milk. Bake at 400°F for 30 minutes or until crust is golden.

Oxtail Stew

During the 1960s I was part owner of a coffee shop situated in a bowling alley on the windward side of Oʻahu. The coffee shop offered a typical breakfast menu of eggs with ham, bacon or luncheon meat, and pancakes. For lunch and dinner, hamburger steak with gravy, roast pork or chicken, rarely roast beef (too expensive), chili with hotdog, beef stew or curry were offered. Every so often, we featured Oxtail stew on the menu. Until then, I had never tasted this dish but I eventually acquired a taste for it.

Over the years, bowling alley menus have advanced far beyond the simple fare we were offering at our coffee shop. I've seen some restaurants offer such gourmet items as furikake salmon and garlic shrimp. Fancy!

Dredge oxtails in flour; brown lightly in large pot on all sides in hot oil. Add onions and garlic; brown lightly. Add water and bay leaves; bring to a boil; cover and simmer 1½ to 2 hours or until oxtails are tender. Add remaining ingredients; simmer additional 30 minutes or until vegetables are done. Thicken with flour-water paste, if desired. Adjust taste as necessary.

YIELD: ABOUT 4-6 SERVINGS

- 4-5 pounds oxtail, disjointed and fat removed
- 1 cup flour
- ½ cup salad oil
- 2 medium onions, wedged
- 1 clove garlic, chopped
- 5 cups water (more if necessary)
- 2 bay leaves
- 1½ teaspoons salt
- ¼ teaspoon pepper
- 2 cans (8 oz. each) tomato sauce
- 1 can (10¾ oz.) can condensed tomato soup
- 4 small carrots, cut into 1-inch pieces
- 4 small potatoes, pared and quartered
- 1 cup sliced celery
- Flour-water mixture for thickening, optional

Shibi No Tataki *(Blackened Tuna)*

ataki, which means "beating in the flavor," is a dish of Japanese origin. Thick tuna fillet strips are quickly seared, cooled, and cut into slices. The rim of the fish is cooked but the center should remain cold and red, making it colorful and attractive. Various condiments are sprinkled on the fish, then lightly tapped with the broadside of a knife before cooking, and served with a prepared sauce.

YIELD: ABOUT 6 SERVINGS

1 to 1½ pounds fresh 'ahi fillet,
    cut into 1-inch blocks
Salt to taste
1 jar (1.9 oz.) nori komi furikake
    (Japanese seasoned
    seaweed mix)
½ cup minced green onion

SAUCE:

¾ cup rice vinegar
¼ cup sugar
1 teaspoon salt
2 tablespoons mirin
1 tablespoon soy sauce
1 teaspoon dashi-no-moto

Season fish strips with salt. Sear fish quickly over high heat in hot nonstick skillet on all sides until surface turns white. Watch carefully so that not more than ⅛-inch cooks through on all 4 sides of fish fillet; center should still be cold and red. Remove fish from skillet and immerse immediately into iced water. Drain, pat dry, wrap in plastic wrap and refrigerate.

About 1 hour before serving, cut fillet into ⅜-inch rectangular slices and arrange like fallen dominoes on serving platter; pat with broadside of knife. Spoon part of the Sauce over fish and pat again. Sprinkle furikake and green onion over fish slices; sprinkle lightly with salt if desired; pat lightly and serve with Sauce.

TO PREPARE SAUCE: Mix all ingredients together until well blended.

Okinawa Imo Manju
(Okinawan Sweet Potato Cakes)

I can remember that on our way home from Japanese language school, a stop at a neighborhood mom and pop store to buy these delicious, flaky snacks was a must for my friends and me. More than 50 years have since passed and I still find these pastries sold at some of the okazu-ya—and as delicious as ever!

Cook sweet potatoes in water to cover in a covered saucepan until soft. Peel; mash with a potato masher or pastry blender (do not use electric mixer). Add butter, milk and sugar; mix well and set aside.

Combine Crust ingredients; stir until mixed well and form into small, walnut-sized balls. Working on a piece of waxed paper, flatten each ball into a small round. Place a ball of Filling in center of crust; gather crust together around Filling and pinch to seal. Place seam side down on ungreased cookie sheet. Flatten slightly with the palm of your hand. Brush tops with milk. If desired, make a dot in the center of each manju using chopstick dipped in food coloring. Bake at 350°F for 30 minutes or until golden brown.

YIELD: 16-18 PIECES

FILLING:

2-3 Okinawan sweet potatoes
Water
2 tablespoon butter
2 tablespoons milk
3 tablespoons sugar

CRUST:

2 ½ cups flour
2 tablespoons sugar
¾ cup canola oil
6 tablespoons ice cold water

TOPPING:

Milk
Red or green food coloring,
    if desired

Mai Tai Chiffon Pie

A sweet rum drink meaning "good" or "out of this world," the Mai Tai has become synonymous with Hawai'i. At your next get-together, surprise your guests with slices of this exotic pie topped with cherries, mint and maybe even an orchid blossom or two atop the whipped cream.

Soften gelatin with water. Beat egg yolks until thickened in saucepan. Blend in ½ cup sugar, salt and Mai Tai mix; cook over low heat, stirring constantly, until mixture thickens. Remove from heat; add softened gelatin and stir until gelatin is thoroughly dissolved. Stir in rum, lemon zest and food coloring; chill until mixture begins to thicken. Beat egg whites until soft peaks form; gradually add the ⅓ cup sugar beating until stiff peaks form. Gently fold the chilled mixture into the egg whites. Pour into baked pie shell and chill until firm, about 2 hours. Top with sweetened whipped cream; garnish with cherries, mint and orchid.

TIP: Mai Tai Mix: ⅓ ounce oregeat syrup, ⅓ ounce Rock Candy syrup and ⅓ ounce orange curacao (Bols).

YIELD: 8 SERVINGS

1 tablespoon unflavored gelatin
¼ cup water
3 eggs, separated
½ cup sugar
½ teaspoon salt
3 tablespoons liquid Mai Tai mix
¼ cup blended Mai Tai rum
1¼ teaspoons lemon zest
2 to 3 drops red food coloring
⅓ cup sugar
9-inch baked pie shell

GARNISHES:

1 cup sweetened whipped cream
6 candied or maraschino cherries, chopped
Sprig of mint
Vanda or dendrobium orchid blossoms, optional

Oahu Market...
An Open Market

(Ian Gillespie)

Constructed of cement, iron and glass and featuring marble top counters, Oahu Market was declared "one of the most sanitary buildings of its kind in the city" when it was opened for business on July 2, 1904 on the corner of King and Kekaulike Streets. The stalls rented for $15 a month and vendors offered such items as fish, meats, vegetables and fruits, at prices less than those available from door-to-door peddlers.

On July 7, 1904 the Pacific Commercial Advertiser noted: "Thousands of Chinese and Japanese patronize the fish stalls and the natives divide their purchases equally between the fish dealers and the owners of meat stalls." In those days, many purchases were wrapped in ti leaves with the stems being so arranged that it could be used as a handle.

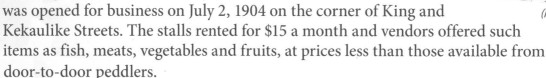

Though many of the vendors have since changed, Oahu Market continues to provide Honolulu with fresh fish, meat, poultry and produce. It stands as a landmark, the last of Honolulu's old open market. Today's open markets and farmers' markets feature more produce, some baked goods and homemade preserves—seldom will you see fresh fish, meat and poultry. The times have changed. However, in remembrance of the "good old days," following is a simple family recipe for chicken.

(Ian Gillespie)

Teriyaki Chicken Wings

This recipe fills me with nostalgia, making me remember small-kid-time. I wonder how many chickens my cousin sold from his Chicken Cradle stall at Oahu Market, which he only recently retired? I wonder how many eggs my cousins packed on the farm they had at one time on Halemaumau Road? I wonder how many chicks were hatched in their hatchery? Gone are the good old days.

Cut tips off chicken wings. Peel taro; cut into quarters or halves. Combine Sauce ingredients; heat to dissolve sugar. Add chicken and taro; cover and bring to a boil over medium heat. Turn heat down to low and simmer for 30 to 45 minutes, stirring occasionally. Add green onion; turn heat off. Delicious with hot, steamed rice.

YIELD: ABOUT 6 SERVINGS

2 pounds chicken wings
6-8 Japanese taro (dasheen)
1 stalk green onion, chopped

SAUCE:

⅔ cup soy sauce
½ cup brown sugar, packed
¼ cup sake (rice wine)
**½ teaspoon fresh grated
   ginger root**

Remembering...

*I*n the early stages of compiling this book, hours were spent sifting through favorite recipes, old and new. Nostalgia exacted a great pull on the taste buds; many of the dishes considered evoked memories not just of taste but also of bygone times, places, and people. While it was difficult to leave out some old favorites, what remains is the absolute best. The following recipes represent a broad spectrum of interesting flavors to be found in Hawai'i. Some of these dishes are stunners perfect for special celebrations, others are simple, everyday favorites. We hope that you'll enjoy our journey back in time as much as we did and that you'll share in our favorites.

All recipes are printed as previously published with minor editing. As all the recipes are those of other cooks, the results are not guaranteed. However, each recipe has stood the test of time and every effort has been made to ensure that each recipe retains its original personality and flavor.

*Restaurants on the beach lured many diners, 1953
(Pono Studio, Kapa'a)*

A Salute to Chef Martin Wyss…
From Your Hawai'i 'Ohana

FOR MORE THAN 40 YEARS OF EXCELLENT FOOD, FINE DINING, AND FRIENDSHIP

Anyone who dined out in the 1980s will recall the Swiss Inn at Niu Valley Shopping Center. In those days, Niu Valley was still considered the country by some, and a drive from far away Mililani or Kailua to eat there was not out of the question.

Chef and owner Martin Wyss, born in Wadneswil, Switzerland, dreamed of becoming a great chef after listening to his brother tell stories of a friend who had traveled the world as a cook. Spurred on by these fabulous tales, the young man sought out and found a chef's apprenticeship in his native country at the age of 16. That apprenticeship enabled Chef Wyss to travel to Spain and then on to Montreal, after finding work as a cook on passenger cruise ships.

Chef Wyss eventually found his way to Hawai'i and the Kahala Hilton, where he became Executive Chef at the age of twenty-six. After a distinguished eighteen-year career at the hotel, Chef Wyss left to open the Swiss Inn with his wife Jeanie.

40

The Swiss Inn embodied several of Chef Wyss' ideals for a successful restaurant—fresh ingredients, great food, a fair price, and a friendly atmosphere, which resulted in a simplicity of flavor that was increasingly hard to find at other restaurants where food was becoming more complicated, fused, mixed and involved multi-step preparations.

Although the original intent was to serve strictly European food, the menu quickly incorporated local favorites and touches. Arthur Murray insisted on fresh local fish, not imported trout, and the pantry manager was adamant that the restaurant needed to have garlic shrimp on the menu. The Wyss' kept the Swiss Inn until 2000, when Martin decided to retire. Following his retirement, he was honored with several accolades honoring his years of service and devotion to his craft, including two Lifetime Achievement Awards: the Chef de Cuisine and National Association of Catering Executive in 2001, and in 2003 from the Hawai'i Culinary Hall Of Fame– Culinary Institute of the Pacific Leeward Community College.

Their famous salad dressing, originated by Martin's mother and bottled as the Swiss Inn Salad Dressing, is still sold in Hawai'i grocery stores.

(Martin Wyss)

In 1979, to celebrate the 75th anniversary of the Gas Company, Muriel and Martin teamed up for an NBC cooking demo (Muriel Miura)

skillet; a
them ever
until almo
nutes.

illet, heat
spoon butte
mushroom
ne and lem
to reduce l
ushrooms a
scallops; m
well. Sprinkle with chopp
parsley and serve. It may
garnished with 1 lemon c
into 2 stars, sprig of parsl
and 2 cherry tomato
slightly sauteed. Makes
servings.

Fish With
Caper Sauce

8 pieces (3 ounces each) op
kapaka, mahimahi or any wh
fish
Salt
Flour
¼ cup unsalted butter
½ lemon
1 tablespoon capers
1 teaspoon chopped parsley
½ cup beef consomme (ava
able in supermarkets)

Season fish with salt a
dust lightly with flour. He
oil or butter in a skillet a
saute the fish slowly, bei
careful not to brown it t
much. When fish is almo

both sides
crisp and golden. Makes
servings.

Scallops
With Peppercorns

1 pound scallops

Swiss Inn a dream come true for Wyss

By Patsy Matsuura
Advertiser Food Editor

One of the most popular eating places on Oahu is the Swiss Inn, a charming little restaurant in the heart of Niu Valley Shopping Center. Nestled between a Chinese restaurant on the left and an Italian restaurant on the right, it's a cozy and comfortable place — one that appeals to local people.

Its owner [...] down-to-ear[...] Before openi[...] executive ch[...] years.

"It's every [...] he began. "A[...] lunch place s[...] family. But w[...] was just right,

From the ve[...] advertised in t[...] customers did t[...] their friends an[...] is good and the[...] keep coming ba[...] spread the news

"That's why w[...] especially the lo[...] have to please. [...] from the tourist [...] comes from Islan[...] the high cost of [...] try to serve them[...] price."

At first Wyss specialized mostly in veal dishes, but soon his customers began to request seafood

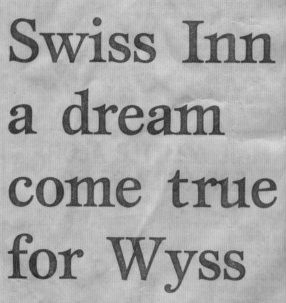

(Martin Wyss)

Advertiser photo by Carl Viti

[...] his specialties — Veal Emince. In the foreground [...] corns and Roesti Potatoes.

[...]mers was Arthur Murray, [...] to ask, "What's the fish [...] cent of the requests are [...] up on fresh seafood [...] door daily.

[...] popular dish. His Veal [...] tyle, for instance, is [...] veal in a light white [...] sauce.

[...]lions Florentine, tender [...] pinach topped with [...] with Swiss cheese.

Wyss said he doesn't spend time putting fancy trimmings on the plates like some high-class restaurants. He prefers the food itself to be

See Swiss Inn, Page F3

basic cooking — nothing [...] cy, but it's the simple [...] ations that keep draw[...] customers to his restaur[...]

Here Wyss shares som[...] his favorite dishes tha[...] easy to prepare.

Veal Emince

9 ounces veal, sliced ver[...]
ly
1½ tablespoons finely ch[...]
round onion
¼ cup fresh mushr[...]
sliced
2 tablespoons butter
1 tablespoon flour
½ cup heavy cream
¼ cup white wine
¼ cup brown sauce (mix[...]
able in supermarkets)
1 teaspoon chopped parsl[...]
Salt, white pepper to tas[...]

Season veal with sal[...] pepper and sprinkle [...] flour. Heat butter in sk[...] until very hot. Add vea[...] saute very fast until sli[...] brown on all sides. Re[...] veal.

Add onion, then m[...] rooms. Saute 1 minute [...] white wine, cream [...] brown sauce and simme[...] minute more. Add vea[...] sauce. Mix well, but do[...] boil. Sprinkle with cho[...] parsley. Serve with R[...] Potatoes (recipe bel[...] Makes 2 servings.

Roesti Potatoes

¼ cup butter
1 teaspoon chopped oreg[...]
½ slice bacon, chopped
1 cup hash browns [...]
cooked potato)

Heat butter in flat sk[...] add onion and bacon. Sa[...] few minutes and add [...] browns. Mix and pat [...] round on bottom of sk[...] Brown evenly on both [...] until crisp and golden. M[...] 2 servings.

Scallops With Peppercorns

1 pound scallops
Salt and pepper to tast[...]
Flour for dusting
¼ cup butter
1½ teaspoons chopped [...]
lots
3 medium fresh mushroo[...]
2 teaspoons green Madi[...]
car peppercorn, lightly cru[...]
(available in supermarkets[...]
2 tablespoons sauterne [...]
1 tablespoon lemon juic[...]
1 teaspoon chopped parsl[...]

Season scallops with [...] and pepper. Dust lightly [...] flour. Melt 3 tablespoo[...]

Each month The Advertiser Food Section will spotlight a Hawaii chef who has won recognition for an outstanding way with food.

Roesti Potatoes
Swiss Inn

*O*wner-Chef, Martin Wyss likes to serve Roesti Potatoes, a Swiss version of the American hash browns, with Veal Emince—a perfect combination of flavors!

Heat non-stick flat skillet; add oil, bacon and butter. When the bacon is ¾ cooked, add onions and sauté for another minute. Add hash browns; add salt and pepper to taste and sauté for 2 minutes or so. Mix and pat into round in skillet. Brown evenly on both sides until crisp and golden. Slide onto platter and sprinkle with chopped parsley.

YIELD: 4 SERVINGS

2 tablespoons canola oil
2 slices bacon, chopped
2 tablespoons butter
2 tablespoons round onion, chopped
4 cups frozen hash browns
Salt and pepper to taste
1 teaspoon chopped parsley

Welcome
to the

"En Guete"
Martin and Jeanie Wyss
Sharon Fuji

(Martin Wyss)

Swiss Inn Kitchen (Martin Wyss)

Veal Emince *(Emince De Veau Zurich Style)*
Swiss Inn

Chef Martin Wyss prepared many scrumptious entrees over the years for Hawai'i diners at his Swiss Inn Restaurant. One widely beloved favorite is this delectable Veal Emince.

YIELD: 4 SERVINGS

18 ounces veal, very thinly sliced
Salt and white pepper to taste
1 tablespoon flour
2 tablespoons oil
1 tablespoon butter
3 tablespoons finely chopped onion
1 cup sliced fresh mushrooms, cooked; or 4 ounces canned mushrooms (stems and pieces)
½ cup white wine
½ cup heavy cream
1 cup brown sauce* or au jus
1 teaspoon chopped parsley

* Brown sauce made from packaged gravy mix may be used.

(Martin Wyss)

Season veal with salt and pepper; sprinkle with flour. Heat oil in skillet until very hot; add butter. Add veal and sauté very quickly until slightly brown on all sides. Add onions and sauté a little longer. Remove veal and onions. Add white wine and mushrooms to hot pan; cook additional 1 to 2 minutes. Add cream and brown sauce. Continue cooking until sauce is reduced to desired consistency (not too thick or thin). Add veal and onion back to sauce. Mix well, but do not boil. Sprinkle with chopped parsley and serve with Roesti Potatoes (see page 43) or linguine noodles.

VARIATIONS: Use boneless, skinless chicken breast or thighs or lean pork, very thinly sliced, instead of veal.

Trout Caprice
Swiss Inn

*U*pon entering
*Chef Wyss'
Swiss Inn, guests would
be greeted warmly by
Martin's wife, Jeanie, and
her sister, Sharon Fujii.
Once seated they would
be treated to amazing
meals like this delicious
Trout Caprice.*

(Martin Wyss)

TO PREPARE MUSHROOM SAUCE: Place mushrooms, white wine, lemon juice, chicken base, and white pepper in saucepan; bring to a boil. Simmer over medium heat until mushrooms are tender and cooked through. Remove from heat and set aside. In another saucepan, make a roux: melt butter over low heat, whisk in flour, stirring constantly. Strain mushroom liquid into roux; bring to a boil and add cream, mushrooms, Maggi and simmer gently for a few minutes. Check seasoning; add salt and white pepper if necessary. Set aside; keep warm.

FOR FISH PREPARATION: Season fish fillets with salt and lemon juice. Dust with flour and dip in egg; sauté in butter or oil 1 to 2 minutes. Place fish on mushroom sauce. Saute bananas in 1 tablespoon butter or canola oil and place on top of fish. For extra flavor and calories, pour a little brown butter over it, if desired. Sprinkle with chopped parsley and garnish with lemon wedge.

YIELD: 4 SERVINGS

MUSHROOM SAUCE:

½ pound mushrooms, cleaned and sliced thin
¼ cup white wine
Few drops lemon juice
1 chicken bouillon cube or scant teaspoon chicken base
Pinch white pepper
1 tablespoon butter or canola oil
1½ tablespoons flour
¼ cup whipping cream
Few drops Maggi* seasoning
Salt and white pepper to taste

FISH:

8 pieces (2-3 oz. each) trout fillet (or mahimahi, sole, perch, or snapper)
Salt to taste
Lemon juice
Flour
2 eggs, beaten
½ stick butter or 2 tablespoons canola oil
2 bananas, sliced lengthwise, quartered
Mushroom Sauce (recipe above)

GARNISH:

Chopped parsley
Lemon wedges

* Maggi seasoning is a brand of bouillon cubes found at most supermarkets.

Welcome
to the

Swiss Inn

"En Guete"

Martin and Jeanie Wyss
Sharon Fujii

Celery Seed Dressing
Maile Room ~ Kahala Hilton

Family affair
Martin Wyss, executive chef at Kahala Hilton Hotel, wins the undaunted approval of daughter Suzie with a taste of one of his holiday pies. A harvest of Wyss' family favorites presides over Thanksgiving Day menus at the hotel's Holiday Award Maile restaurant and the oceanside Hala Terrace. Phone 734-2211 for reservations.

(Martin Wyss)

A delicious dressing from Chef Martin Wyss, it was served with the Maile Salad at the Kahala Hilton Hotel. The Maile Salad called for a generous bed of Mānoa lettuce, sprinkled with chopped celery and bay shrimps then topped with two scoops of firm-ripe avocado on each serving.

YIELD: ABOUT 6 CUPS

1 cup cider vinegar
¾ cup mayonnaise
⅔ cup French's mustard
½ cup sugar
1½ teaspoons celery seed
2 tablespoons salt
¾ teaspoon black pepper
1 tablespoon garlic
2 tablespoons chopped or grated onion
1 tablespoon Worchestershire sauce
1 tablespoon lemon juice
1½ teaspoons Maggi* seasoning
3 cups vegetable oil

* Maggi seasoning is a brand of bouillon cubes found at most supermarkets.

Whisk all ingredients, except oil, together in large bowl 30 seconds or until well-blended. Slowly add oil, stirring or whisking continuously. Store in covered jar and keep refrigerated. Shake well before serving.

Remembering…

Tournedos Madagascar
Maile Room ~ Kahala Hilton

This dish, created by Chef Martin Wyss, was very popular amongst diners at the elegant Maile Room. The sauce, perfectly spiced with Madagascar peppercorns, is best served over the sautéed fillet of beef.

Heat 2 tablespoons of the butter in skillet. Sauté fillets on both sides until medium rare. Remove to plate.

Melt remaining 2 tablespoons butter in skillet. Finely chop 1 tablespoon shallot, sauté slightly; add peppercorns and white wine; reduce a little. Add brown sauce and heavy cream. Simmer until sauce has a nice consistency. Add chopped parsley to sauce and pour over fillets. Sprinkle with remaining shallot and parsley. Serve immediately.

TIP: Dry green peppercorns are readily available in most markets these days. Soak in water for an hour to reconstitute before using in this recipe.

YIELD: 2 SERVINGS

4 tablespoons butter
¾ pound beef fillet, cut into 4 pieces
2 tablespoons chopped shallots
1 teaspoon green Madagascar peppercorns,* slightly crushed
3 tablespoons white wine
⅓ cup packaged instant brown sauce (prepare according to directions)
⅓ cup heavy cream
Chopped parsley

* *Madagascar peppercorns are found at most supermarkets.*

Chef Gordy Dambach presenting Martin the Lifetime Achievement Award in 2001
(Martin Wyss)

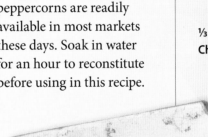

(Muriel Miura)

Remembering... 49

Easy Char Siu Bao *(Pork-Filled Rolls)*

YIELD: 8-10 SERVINGS

1 (10⅓ oz.) can refrigerated
   biscuits or dinner rolls

FILLING:

1 cup char siu (sweet roast
   pork)
¼ cup minced green onion
½ teaspoon soy sauce
Dash of pepper

2 tablespoons salad oil

As a youngster, I often anxiously awaited the "call" of the Manapua Man on Saturdays as he walked past our home to sell his delicious dim sum snacks from the two five-gallon metal cans he balanced on a pole slung over his shoulders. I can still hear him calling "Manapua, pepeiao!" In addition to manapua, he also offered pepeiao, half moon and siu mai.

Manapua became popular among plantation workers during the early years of the twentieth-century. The name, manapua, is a shortened, pidgin version of the Hawaiian name mea ʻono puaʻa, which means "delicious things filled with pork." Today, manapua can be found filled with various ingredients such as chicken, turkey, vegetables, and lup cheong. There is even breakfast manapua filled with eggs, SPAM®, and cheese. Some restaurants offer such a wide variety of manapua, color-coded with an accompanying list explaining what each little steamed bun, or bao, is filled with. There are Hawaiian-style fillings such as kālua pork, and sweet dessert-like fillings such as coconut or Chinese black sugar. Whatever your palate may lean towards, there's sure to be a hot, steaming manapua there to satisfy it.

Combine filling ingredients and mix thoroughly. Place 1 tablespoon filling in center of each circle of dough. Pinch edges together to seal. Brush tops with salad oil. Steam, seam side down, in waxed paper-lined steamer for 15-20 minutes.

TIP: Rolls may also be baked at 375°F for 10 minutes or until golden.

Manapua Man, circa 1960 (Hawaiʻi State Archives)

Dungeness Crab Legs Sauté
Alioto's ~ Honolulu

A favorite recipe from a bygone restaurant, this crab recipe was once featured on the menu of Alioto's. The restaurant has been gone for years, but this delicious and easy-to-prepare recipe remains.

Sauté mushrooms light in hot oil. Add garlic and sauté until garlic turns golden brown. Immediately add white wine and let reduce. Add crab legs. While sautéing, add lemon juice, brown sauce and salt. Finish off with parsley and butter. Sauté until butter is blended evenly.

YIELD: 4 SERVINGS

4 medium mushrooms, sliced
1 tablespoon salad oil
1 small clove garlic, finely
    chopped
5 ounces (10 tablespoons)
    white wine
24 Dungeness crab legs
Juice of ½ lemon
1 tablespoon brown sauce*
Pinch of salt
1 teaspoon chopped parsley
2 heaping tablespoons butter

* Brown sauce made from packaged gravy mix may be used.

Waioli Guava Dressing
Waioli Tea Room~ Honolulu

Waioli Tea Room, circa 1924 (Hawai'i State Archives)

Established in 1922 by the Salvation Army, the Waioli Tea Room's original mission was to teach girls the fundamentals of homemaking. A grass hut, is situated on the grounds. This hut was originally at Aina Hau, the Waikīkī home of Princess Kaiulani and the hut is purported to have been author Robert Louis Stevenson's meeting place with the princess and her friends for many story-telling sessions.

Combine all ingredients and beat with rotary beater until well-blended. Chill. Serve over fresh island greens.

YIELD: ABOUT 3¼ CUPS

1 cup mayonnaise
1 cup tomato catsup
¼ cup vinegar
½ cup salad oil
1 teaspoon dry mustard
2 teaspoons lemon juice
½ cup guava jelly or jam
½ teaspoon garlic salt

Waioli Dressing

Combine all ingredients in quart jar; cover and shake vigorously until well mixed. Refrigerate and let stand for a day before serving over fresh island greens.

YIELD: ABOUT 3½ CUPS

1 cup olive or vegetable oil
¾ cup sugar or honey
2 teaspoons paprika
Dash of cayenne
3 teaspoons salt
¼ cup wine vinegar (white or red)
2 cloves garlic, mashed
1 cup catsup
3 teaspoons dry mustard
1 teaspoon MSG, optional

Chocolate Crème Dessert
Top Of The Fair ⁓ New York, 1965

Although this is not an Island recipe, I thought that I would share it here. It reminds me of my time as a guest demonstrator at the New York World's Fair in 1965. While there, my daughter and I first sampled this scrumptious dessert. This always evokes the many fond memories of the sights, sounds, exhibits and food of that fabulous fair!

YIELD: 6-8 SERVINGS

⅔ cup sugar
2 tablespoons cornstarch
1 tablespoon unflavored
   gelatin
¼ teaspoon salt
2 cups milk
2 squares (2 oz.) unsweetened
   chocolate
3 eggs, separated
1 teaspoon vanilla extract
1 cup sweetened whipped
   cream
Chocolate curls
Maraschino cherries

Combine ⅓ cup sugar with cornstarch, gelatin and salt. Blend in milk; add chocolate. Cook over medium heat, stirring constantly, until mixture thickens and comes to a boil. Turn heat off; stir small amount of hot mixture into slightly beaten egg yolks; blend into hot mixture. Bring to a boil; cook and stir 1 minute. Cool.

Beat egg whites and vanilla extract until soft peaks form. Gradually add remaining ⅓ cup sugar; beat until stiff peaks form. Fold in chocolate mixture gradually, blending well. Chill until Chocolate Crème mounds slightly when spooned. Dish into sherbet or dessert glasses. Garnish each with whipped cream, chocolate curls and maraschino cherry. Chill thoroughly before serving.

Muriel and daughter, Shari, at NY World's Fair, 1965 (Muriel Miura)

FESTIVAL of GAS

NEW YORK WORLD'S FAIR 1964-1965

BIG TOP CAROUSEL — HOUSE OF ENERGY — APPLIANCE GARDEN
THEATER OF FOOD — ENERGY CENTER — FERRIS WHEEL
GASLIGHT PATIO — FESTIVAL RESTAURANT
GAS INDUSTRY CLUB

Mushu Pork (a.k.a. Chinaman's Hat)
Maple Garden

Though late restaurateur and dear friend, Robert Hsu is no longer with us, he left behind a wonderful legacy of delicious Mandarin food served at the exquisite Maple Garden. Robert was also generous with his recipes. Here's an excellent one.

Stir-fry pork in hot oil over high heat 1 minute or until cooked. Add won bok, bamboo shoot, black fungus, straw mushroom, chive, long rice and bean sprouts; stir-fry over high heat 20 to 30 seconds. Season with soy sauce, pepper and sherry; stir-fry additional 1 minute. Make paste of cornstarch and water; add to filling mixture with sesame oil; cook until thickened. Place on large serving platter.

Fry eggs into thin omelet, 8-inches in diameter, in non-stick skillet and place on top of cooked filling.

To serve, spread 2 teaspoons hoisin sauce on tortilla and place 2 to 3 tablespoons filling on top. Roll, like for jelly roll, tucking sides in, if desired.

YIELD: 6 SERVINGS

FILLING:

½ pound lean pork, julienned
2 tablespoons cottonseed or salad oil
1 leaf won bok, cut into julienne strips
2 tablespoons bamboo shoot, cut into julienne strips
2 tablespoons black fungus, softened in water and cut into strips
1 tablespoon minced chives
2 tablespoons long rice, softened in water and chopped
2 tablespoons bean sprouts

1 tablespoon soy sauce
1 teaspoon white pepper
1 tablespoon cooking sherry
1 tablespoon cornstarch
1 tablespoon water
1 tablespoon sesame oil

3 eggs, beaten slightly
6 flour tortilla
Prepared hoisin sauce*

* Available in Oriental food section of most markets.

(Mutual Publishing)

'Ōpakapaka Meuniere
Rex's Restaurant

YIELD: 2 SERVINGS

2 pieces (6 oz. each) 'ōpakapaka fillets
Flour
4 eggs, beaten
2 tablespoons butter
½ cup white wine
Juice of 1 lemon
Pinch of minced shallots
Pinch of minced garlic
1 tablespoon chopped parsley
2 tablespoons Hollandaise sauce*

* Hollandaise sauce prepared from packaged mix may be used.

Here's a simple recipe for one of Hawai'i's favorite fish. If 'ōpakapaka, the gray snapper, is not available, any other snapper or sea bass may be used.

Lightly flour 'ōpakapaka fillets and dip them in beaten eggs. Shake off excess egg and cook in melted butter over medium heat. Add white wine, lemon juice, shallots, garlic and parsley; reduce to ¼ cup liquid. Remove fillets from pan. Let liquid cool. Add Hollandaise sauce and blend.

Summit Spinach Salad
The Summit ~ Ala Moana Americana Hotel

YIELD: 6 SERVINGS

12 bunches spinach, washed and
    trimmed
½ pound bacon, cut into fine crosswise
    strips
½ cup olive oil
⅓ cup cider vinegar
1 tablespoon sugar
Salt and pepper to taste
½ medium round onion, minced
1 clove garlic, minced

Another lovely restaurant that offered a spectacular view of the ocean and Waikīkī was The Summit, which sat atop the Ala Moana Americana Hotel which is adjacent to the renowned Ala Moana Shopping Center. It was known for its fine dining menu as well as its impeccable service.

Place spinach in wooden bowl; set aside. Saute bacon in skillet until crispy; pour off excess fat then stir in olive oil, vinegar, sugar, salt, pepper, onion and garlic and bring to a boil. Pour hot mixture over spinach. Gently turn spinach a couple of times to coat. Serve while warm.

Snowballs
Dutch Girl Pastry Shoppes

There was a time when one could always find a variety of freshly baked cookies, such as Snowballs (a.k.a. Russian Tea Cookies or Mexican Wedding Cakes), at the Dutch Girl Pastry Shoppes, located in the Liliha/Palama area. The cookies weren't packaged in crisp cello bags. They were simply found in a glass cookie jar, securely covered with a lid and situated on the counters of bakeries or corner grocery stores. When purchased, the cookies were plucked from the jar with a pair of chopsticks or tongs (sometimes even by hand) and wrapped in a little white paper bag. A great treat!

Circa 1961 (Young Family)

Cream together butter, sugar and vanilla extract until fluffy. Mix together flour and salt; add to the creamed mixture, blending thoroughly. Add nuts and mix well. Shape into 1-inch balls and place on baking sheets lined with parchment paper. Bake at 325°F for 15 to 20 minutes or until set. Do not brown. Cool; then roll in confectioner's sugar. Store in airtight container.

YIELD: ABOUT 6 DOZEN

1 cup butter, softened
½ cup sugar
2 teaspoons vanilla extract
2 cups flour, sifted
½ teaspoon salt
2 cups finely chopped nuts (macadamia, pecans, walnuts)
Confectioner's sugar

Sesame Chicken Orientale
La Mancha Restaurant

A simple recipe found in our archives, this dish offers a novel variation on teriyaki chicken. This recipe is relatively easy to make and uses readily available ingredients, but the flavor is complex and satisfying.

YIELD: 4-5 SERVINGS

2 pounds boneless chicken
   breasts
1 tablespoon sherry
½ cup soy sauce
1 tablespoon sesame oil
1 tablespoon toasted sesame
   seeds
½ cup flour
1 cup cornstarch
6 tablespoons brown sugar
3 large eggs
3 teaspoons minced garlic
2 teaspoons minced shallots
2 stalks green onion, minced
2 teaspoons grated fresh
   ginger

Combine all ingredients, except chicken, in large bowl and mix thoroughly. Place the chicken in the batter making sure that each piece is completely coated; cover the bowl and refrigerate overnight or at least 8 hours. Deep-fry in oil heated to 350 to 375°F. until golden brown on both sides and done. Drain on absorbent paper and serve immediately.

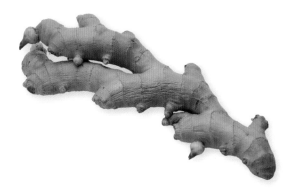

Shrimp Tempura
Columbia Inn

*C*omfort food was always in abundant supply at the old Columbia Inn, formerly located on Kapiolani Blvd. Owned by Tosh Kaneshiro's family, Columbia Inn was known for its sports bar and family style menu, featuring local favorites like Chef George Uyehara's Shrimp Tempura.

In a large bowl, mix water, salt and egg. (Water must be ice-cold or tempura will not be very crispy.) Mix well. Add cornstarch, cake flour and food coloring; mix until well blended. Heat oil to 375°F. Dip a shrimp in batter and deep fry 1 to 2 minutes or until golden brown. Remove from oil and drain on paper towels. Repeat with remaining shrimps. Serve hot with dipping sauce.

TO PREPARE DIPPING SAUCE: Combine shrimp with water in small saucepan; simmer over low heat for 25 minutes to get flavor of shrimp; strain broth with sieve and discard shrimp. Add soy sauce and sugar. Season to taste with salt.

TIPS: Fresh fish fillets, other seafood and fresh vegetables of your choice may also be dipped in the batter to make tempura.

(Muriel Miura)

YIELD: 4-6 SERVINGS

2 cups ice-cold water
1 teaspoon salt
1 egg
¼ cup cornstarch
2 cups cake flour
2 or 3 drops yellow food
    coloring
16 to 20 shrimp, shelled,
    deveined and butterflied
Oil for deep frying

DIPPING SAUCE:

¼ cup dry shrimp*
2 cups water
2 tablespoons soy sauce
½ teaspoon sugar, optional
Salt to taste

* Dashi-no-moto base may be used instead of dry shrimp for the dipping sauce. Follow package directions.

Ilikai Hotel (Hawai'i State Archives)

Fillet of Mahimahi Grilled Saint-Germain
Pier 7 ~ Ilikai Hotel

One of the premier dinner destinations for many visitors to Hawai'i was Pier 7, formerly located at the Ilikai Hotel where one could order good-tasting seafood such as this mahimahi dish.

YIELD: 4 SERVINGS

2 pounds fresh mahimahi fillet
Juice of ½ lemon
1 tablespoon Worcestershire
  sauce
Salt and pepper to taste
¼ cup white bread crumbs
1 tablespoon chopped parsley
English mustard powder
¼ cup butter, melted
White wine

SAUCE:

2 pieces shallots, chopped fine
6 tablespoons unsalted butter
Tarragon leaves
Salt and pepper to taste
Juice of ½ lemon
Worcestershire sauce
2 tablespoons chopped parsley
⅓ pint white wine
⅓ pint fish stock

Slice mahimahi fillet into 8 medallions. Marinate in lemon juice, Worcestershire sauce, salt and pepper to taste.

Mix bread crumbs with parsley and a pinch of English mustard powder. Baste mahimahi (one side only) with butter and cover the same side completely with bread crumb mixture. Place mahimahi in a buttered, oven-proof earthenware or flat pottery dish crumbs side up, and sprinkle with white wine to moisten. Broil for approximately 8 minutes.

TO PREPARE SAUCE: Lightly sauté shallots in 1 tablespoon butter. Add a pinch of tarragon leaves, salt, pepper, lemon juice, few drops of Worcestershire sauce and parsley. Add white wine and fish stock; simmer gently over medium heat until liquid is reduced to half. Remove from heat and whisk in remaining unsalted butter.

Sauce should be served separately. Serve mahimahi in original baking dish. Recommend side serving of crisp tossed green salad with oil and vinegar dressing.

German Cheesecake
Whaler's Broiler ~ Ala Moana Americana Hotel

Though there were a number of restaurants at the Ala Moana Americana Hotel, one of the most popular was the Whaler's Broiler, where one could find this delicious cheesecake.

Combine flour and confectioner's sugar; beat in butter until mixture resembles crumbs. Beat in egg and egg white. Place mixture on a floured board. Roll out sugar crust and place on the base and sides of a greased 10-inch springform pan.

FILLING: Combine cottage cheese and ¾ cup sugar; beat in egg yolks. Gradually add heavy cream, grated lemon and orange zest. Fold flour into mixture. Beat egg whites, gradually adding remaining sugar, until stiff. Fold into cheese mixture. Pour into pastry-lined pan. Bake at 375°F for 40 minutes or until done.

TIP: Place a piece of foil loosely over the top of the cake while baking to prevent it from browning too rapidly.

YIELD: 10-12 SERVINGS

SUGAR CRUST:

1¼ cups flour
7 tablespoons confectioner's sugar
¼ cup butter, softened
1 egg, beaten
1 egg white

FILLING:

1½ pounds (3 cups) cottage cheese
¾ cup sugar
5 egg yolks
½ cup heavy cream
Zest of ½ lemon
Zest of ½ orange
¾ cup flour
5 egg whites
¼ cup sugar

Tobler® Best Ever Muffins
Garden Court ~ Liberty House

In the 1970s, Liberty House's Garden Court was the perfect place for weary shoppers to rest and recover. There one would find a courtesy staff, freshly brewed coffee or tea, and these wonderful, warm Tobler Muffins, which were the perfect "pick-me-up" snack after a long day of shopping.

YIELD: ABOUT 2 DOZEN

½ cup butter, softened
¾ cup sugar
1 teaspoon vanilla extract
3 eggs
1 cup sour cream
2 cups flour
1 teaspoon baking powder
1 teaspoon baking soda
¼ teaspoon salt

TOPPING:

1¼ cups brown sugar, packed
½ cup flour
2 teaspoons cinnamon
¼ cup melted butter
2 bars Tobler®* (3 to 3.52 oz.
   any flavor), chopped

* Tobler® was a brand of chocolate bars sold at Liberty House. However, any chocolate-covered candy bar (e.g., Snickers®, Twix®, etc.) may be substituted.

Cream butter and sugar; beat in eggs and sour cream. In a separate bowl, stir together flour, baking powder, baking soda and salt. Stir in sour cream mixture until dry ingredients are moistened. Fill lined or prepared muffin pans one-half full.

To make topping, combine all topping ingredients and mix until moistened. Sprinkle on top of muffins. Bake at 375°F for 10 to 15 minutes or until tester inserted in center of muffin comes out clean.

(Mutual Publishing)

Chicken Pineapple
La Ronde Restaurant

The story goes that a Seattle architect was credited for inventing the revolving restaurant when he built the Honolulu La Ronde in 1961. Built atop the Ala Moana Building, requiring two elevator rides to get to the top, it took an hour for the restaurant to revolve completely, and was certainly not the place for anyone with a weak stomach. Still, for those patrons with a sterner constitution the restaurant offered delicious cuisine and a breath-taking view of the city.

La Ronde Restaurant, circa 1962 (Bishop Museum)

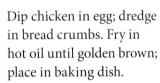

(Joe Kimura, James Kau)

Dip chicken in egg; dredge in bread crumbs. Fry in hot oil until golden brown; place in baking dish.

Combine ingredients for pineapple sauce; mix well and pour over chicken. Bake at 375°F for 30 minutes or until done.

YIELD: 2-4 SERVINGS

4 pieces boneless chicken breasts
1 egg, beaten
½ cup bread crumbs
½ cup salad oil

PINEAPPLE SAUCE:

1 can (8 oz.) pineapple juice
1 cup sugar
2 teaspoons curry powder
Juice of ½ lemon
1 tablespoon cornstarch

Canlis' Shrimps
Canlis' ～ Honolulu

Cooking with dry vermouth was originated by Peter Canlis during World War II when wines were scarce. Following is a tip from Canlis, "Use dry vermouth in any recipe that calls for white wine and you'll notice the improvement in the bouquet and flavor. Also, use a tablespoon of dry vermouth over your steak, chops or fish after they have been cooked…it will make a little Au Jus right on your plate. With lobsters—after you have broiled your lobster face down, turn them over and add a tablespoon of dry vermouth into the shell and let steam for about five minutes."

Into a large skillet place olive oil. When simmering add shrimp and allow to cook until golden brown. Reduce heat and add butter, garlic, salt and pepper. When you think you have too much salt, add more. This is one dish where you cannot over salt.

When well-blended, raise heat to "very hot." Add lemon juice and dry Vermouth; cook for about one minute, constantly stirring or shaking. May be served as an appetizer or entrée.

YIELD: 4-6 ENTRÉE SERVINGS

2 pounds large prawns, shelled leaving tails on
1 ounce olive oil
1 ounce butter
1 small clove garlic, crushed
¼ teaspoon salt
¼ teaspoon fresh ground black pepper
Juice of 2 lemons
2 ounces dry Vermouth

Danish Pudding
Garden Court ∼ Liberty House

A variation on the classic bread pudding, this recipe uses stale Danish pastries in place of bread and it is simply delicious! It was once a featured item on the dessert cart at the Garden Court Restaurant at the late Liberty House. It was one of Executive Chef James Sueyoshi's creations and he generously shared this recipe with me sometime in the sixties. It is the perfect way to use leftovers to create a delicious new dish…try it!

YIELD: 8 SERVINGS

3 cups milk
¾ cup sugar
3 tablespoons melted butter
2 teaspoons vanilla extract
5 eggs, well beaten
**4 cups day-old Danish pastry,
    cut into 1-inch cubes**
Cinnamon
Nutmeg

Combine milk, sugar, butter, vanilla extract and eggs; beat well to combine. Place Danish pastry into 1½-quart casserole or baking pan. Pour egg mixture over; mix and press lightly to moisten Danish pastry. Sprinkle with cinnamon and nutmeg. Bake at 350°F for 45 minutes or until custard is done.

NOTE: Custard is done when knife inserted in center comes out clean.

(Mutual Publishing)

LIBERTY HOUSE

Sashimi Salad
King's Garden

*K*ing's Garden, formerly located on the corner of 10th and Waialae Avenues in Kaimuki, was known for their fine specialty Chinese dishes, the most outstanding of which was their delectable Sashimi Salad. The restaurant was the scene of many a birthday party, reunion, and other family get-togethers. It was a neighborhood institution that is sorely missed, but thanks to Chef Tylun Pang, the legacy of this wonderful, neighborhood restaurant lives on through this recipe.

Slice the fish fillet into thin bite-size strips. Squeeze the juice from the lemon onto the fish slices; marinate for 2 hours. In a large salad bowl, place lettuce, marinated fish and all the remaining julienne-cut vegetables and pickles; set aside or in refrigerator.

PREPARE THE DRESSING: Combine all the ingredients in a bowl; whisk together until all ingredients are well mixed; pour over salad and toss gently. Add fried won ton strips or rice noodles and toss again. Serve garnished with chopped peanuts, Chinese parsley and sesame seeds.

YIELD: ABOUT 4-6 SERVINGS

¾ pound sea bass (hapu'upu'u) or snapper ('ōpakapaka) fillet, boneless and skinless
1 whole lemon, cut in half
1½ tablespoons julienne-cut Chinese sweet pickled scallions (kew tao)
1½ tablespoons julienne-cut Chinese sweet pickled white cucumber (chagwa)
1 tablespoon julienne-cut sweet pickled red ginger (sin geurng)
1½ tablespoons julienne cut fresh young ginger root
¼ cup julienne-cut white radish (daikon)
¼ cup julienne-cut carrot
½ head lettuce or won bok cut into salad bites
2 stalks green onion, cut julienne
1½ cups crispy fried won ton strips or fried rice noodles

DRESSING:

3 tablespoons hoisin sauce
2 tablespoons peanut oil, heat until lightly smoking and fragrant
½ teaspoon dry mustard powder
1 teaspoon sugar
½ teaspoon salt
1 tablespoon sesame oil

GARNISHES:

¼ cup roasted peanuts, chopped
½ bunch Chinese parsley sprigs to garnish
2 teaspoons toasted sesame seeds

Double Fruit-Glazed Pork Chops
Kona Inn ~ Big Island

he old Kona Inn was the setting for a number of wonderful memories. I traveled frequently to the Inn to attend cooking demonstrations. Built in 1928 by the Inter-Island Steam Navigation Co., it was always a wonderful place to relax, look out at the gorgeous Hawaiian sunset and enjoy fine food like these fruit-glazed pork chops.

YIELD: 6 SERVINGS

6 double-rib (6-8 oz. each) pork chops
Salt and pepper to taste

SAUCE:

2 cups brown sugar, packed
½ cup unsweetened pineapple juice
½ cup honey
2 teaspoons dry mustard
6 whole cloves
12 whole coriander seeds, crushed
1 orange, sliced
1 lemon, sliced
1 lime, sliced
6 maraschino cherries

Brown chops in skillet; season with salt and pepper. Place in shallow baking dish. Combine Sauce ingredients; mix well and spoon 3 tablespoons over each chop. Bake, uncovered, at 325°F for 1 to 1¼ hours or until done.

Peg a slice of orange, lemon and lime on every other chop and secure in place with toothpick. Top with maraschino cherry; baste fruits with sauce and bake additional 10 minutes.

Kona Inn, Kailua-Kona, circa 1950s (Hawai'i State Archives)

Green Goddess Dressing
Sky Room ～ Honolulu Airport Terminal

Back in the days when a flight from Honolulu to the West Coast could last upwards of eight hours, it was fashionable for travelers to take a meal before boarding Pan Am's Stratocruiser. Often the restaurant of choice was the Sky Room at the old Honolulu Airport Terminal alongside Keʻehi Lagoon, where this tasty dressing was served.

Combine first 6 ingredients in blender or food processor fitted with steel blade. Blend or process until well pulverized. Stir mixture into mayonnaise and refrigerate until ready to add to torn Mānoa lettuce leaves. This dressing may be kept under refrigeration up to 2 weeks.

YIELD: ABOUT 1 QUART

6 tablespoons tarragon vinegar
6 tablespoons dried tarragon
¼ cup chopped onion
¼ cup chopped green onion
¼ cup chopped parsley
1 can (2 oz.) anchovy fillets
1 quart real mayonnaise

Sky Room, circa 1950 (Bishop Museum)

(Mutual Publishing)

Curried Lobster with Fried Haupia
Golden Dragon ～ Hilton Hawaiian Village

*C*reated by Executive Chef Dai Hoy Chang of the Hilton Hawaiian Village's Golden Dragon, this lobster dish became a popular menu item as diners were attracted to its blend of distinctly flavors of coconut milk and lobster. Though the preparation of this dish is labor intensive, it is well worth the effort.

YIELD: ABOUT 4 SERVINGS

2 tablespoons vegetable oil
3 tablespoons round onion, diced
8 ounces (1½ cups) lobster tail
    meat, cut in 1 ½ inch cubes
¼ cup chicken stock
¼ cup curry powder
¼ cup coconut milk
2 tablespoons half & half cream
Dash of salt and pepper
¼ cup green peas
¼ cup cooked diced carrots
1 small potato, cubed
3 tablespoons raisins
8 deep-fried haupia pieces
    (recipe follows)

CORNSTARCH MIXTURE:

2 tablespoons cornstarch
2 tablespoons chicken stock

Heat 2 tablespoons oil in wok, fry potato 2 minutes or until cooked; remove and set aside.

Heat wok on high heat, add oil, then reduce heat slightly. Stir-fry onion and lobster 2 minutes or until cooked thoroughly. Add chicken stock, curry powder, coconut milk and half & half; stir-fry 1 minute more. Stir the cornstarch mixture into the wok. Add peas, carrots, potato and raisins; cook additional 2 minutes. Place on serving platter. Garnish with fried haupia (recipe follows).

Diners enjoy ocean views from open gazebo overlooking the lagoon
(Hilton Hawaiian Village Resort & Spa)

Fried Haupia

Golden Dragon ∼ Hilton Hawaiian Village

Heat coconut milk in double boiler. Stir together water, sugar and the 5 tablespoons cornstarch until smooth; stir into coconut milk and cook over low heat, mixing constantly, until thickened. Increase heat slightly and stir the mixture continuously to prevent burning. Pour mixture into a cake pan, 8 x 8 x 2-inches. Cool until set.

To garnish curried lobster dish, cut haupia into about 32 diamond shapes, each 1 x 1½ x 1-inch. Otherwise, cut haupia into 24 pieces, each 2 x 1½-inches. Dip each in Egg Wash, dust with cornstarch and deep-fry 2 minutes in hot oil or until light brown. Drain on absorbent paper. Serve with curried lobster.

YIELD: 24-32 PIECES

1½ cups coconut milk
¾ cup water
⅓ cup sugar
5 tablespoons cornstarch
2 tablespoons cornstarch for dusting
Vegetable oil for deep-frying

EGG WASH:

1 egg
1 cup water
1 tablespoon flour

Carving in Golden Dragon retaurant, circa 1958 (Bishop Museum)

Escalopes of Veal with Morels
Champeaux's ~ Ilikai Hotel

ituated atop the Ilikai Hotel, the elegant Champeaux's, with its breathtaking view of the Pacific and wonderful menu, was formerly the destination for a special dining experience. This Escalopes de Veau aux Morels was a specialty of Champeaux's Chef Tylun Pang.

YIELD: ABOUT 2 SERVINGS

4 slices (3 oz. each) boneless
   veal loin
Salt and pepper to taste
Flour to dust
2 tablespoons clarified butter

SAUCE:

1 tablespoon butter
1 tablespoon olive oil
1 tablespoon chopped shallots
½ ounce dried morels, pre-
   soaked in water, split and
   remove sand
½ cup white wine
6 tablespoons veal demi glaze*
3 tablespoons heavy cream
Salt and pepper to taste
1 teaspoon chopped parsley

* You may substitute reduced brown beef stock (low salt) for veal demi glaze.

(Tylun Pang)

Season veal fillets with salt and pepper; lightly dust each slice with flour. Heat clarified butter in sauté pan over moderate heat; sauté veal until evenly browned on both sides. Remove veal and place onto serving platter.

After removing veal from sauté pan, return pan back to the burner to prepare sauce; add butter and olive oil. Add shallots and morels; sauté 1 minute. Deglaze pan with white wine. Add demi glaze and cream; reduce liquid by one-half. Finish the sauce by adjusting seasoning to taste; add chopped parsley. Pour Sauce over sautéed veal escalopes and serve with your favorite potatoes and fresh, cooked vegetables of choice.

TIP: Morels are such a precious treat that they are usually prepared simply in order not to detract from their wonderful earthy essence.

Fire-Pit Basting Sauce
Coco Palms ~ Kaua'i

This recipe came from "the cook" at the historic Coco Palms Hotel. It evokes warm memories of our friends who came to the cooking demonstrations conducted at the Kaua'i War Memorial Convention Center in Līhue during the sixties. This recipe was used both as a marinade and basting sauce for beef roast which was cooked in the oven using the rotisserie feature rather than an open fire-pit—'onolicious!

YIELD: ABOUT 1 ¾ CUPS

⅓ cup soy sauce
½ cup salad oil
½ cup wine vinegar
½ cup lemon juice
1 tablespoon grated ginger root
¼ teaspoon cracked pepper
2 cloves garlic, crushed

Combine all ingredients thoroughly. Use to marinate or baste beef or lamb roasts and steaks.

TIP: 1 teaspoon dry ginger may be substituted for 1 tablespoon grated fresh ginger root.

Omiyage...the Custom of Gift-Giving

The Japanese custom of gift-giving, omiyage, is a way of showing appreciation for those you love when you are traveling far from home. This adopted tradition has been widely embraced by the people of Hawai'i and fits in well with the islands' cullture of aloha and generosity. Gifts that reflect the uniqueness of the islands abound, and edible goodies are the most popular gifts to share. It's a way to share Hawai'i with those who couldn't come, and also a way to bring a little bit of home to transplants on the Mainland and elsewhere yearning for some local treats.

All kinds of "only in Hawai'i" treats can be found: sweet and salty bags of crackseed from the corner store; large baskets of arare, flavored popcorn, and cookies; specialty coffees; boxes of manapua or malasadas; pies; and the ever popular

(Mutual Publishing)

(continued on next page)

chocolate covered macadamia nuts—the list is endless. And there are many ways to make your gift island-specific—chocolate dipped cookies from the Big Island, sweet bread from Moloka'i, candies from Maui. The gift doesn't need to be expensive. Here, omiyage customs tend to be more relaxed with the focus on the thought behind the gift rather than the gift itself. It's also not necessary to follow the many Japanese rules governing the practices of how gifts should be wrapped and given.

Perhaps the most welcome and appreciated gift is the one that's homemade. Why purchase a box of goodies when you can make some using the island's many unique ingredients? From macadamia nuts to edamame to Hawaiian salt to tropical fruits, the list of available ingredients await for you to make the perfect temiyage (casual, small gift) for a homesick loved one. Here, we offer you a selection of recipes that can be made and easily packaged.

Char Siu Rub

har siu is a popular type of flavoring used for many Chinese roasts. Islanders will be most familiar with it as the sweet barbecued roast pork served as a side dish or garnish in many local favorites. Below, Chef Tylun Pang of Maui shares his recipe for Char Siu Rub. This rub can be bottled and given as an omiyage or used to prepare delicious char siu flavored meats.

Combine the fermented red bean curd and hoisin sauce in a large bowl; mix well. Gradually add all the sugar and continue to mix. This will help break down any lumps from the bean curd. Next mix in the white pepper, Chinese five spice powder and the red food color. Continue mixing until all ingredients are incorporated. Store in covered jars in a cool place until ready to use. A pound of this rub should be enough to marinate approximately 5 pounds of meat.

When ready to use, rub the mix generously using disposable gloves onto the meat covering all surfaces well and place the seasoned meat into a sealed bag. Juices from the meat will create a sauce let this marinate for 3 days turning periodically. Meat will be ready to cook on day 3.

When ready to cook, remove meat out of the marinade and place on rack in foil-lined pan to catch the drippings. This will make clean-up easier and not ruin your pan with burnt sugar drippings. Bake at 450°F for 20 minutes. Turn heat down to 350°F. and continue to cook until meat is done (use meat thermometer). Cooking time will depend on the meat selected and size of meat. Brush the meat with honey and serve.

SUGGESTED MEATS: Pork loin, strips of pork butt, baby back ribs, country style ribs, chicken thighs or my favorite turkey tails.

YIELD: ABOUT 25 CUPS

5 pounds sugar
¾ cups salt
2 tablespoons white pepper
2 tablespoons Chinese five-spice powder*
¼ cup fermented red bean curd (nam yui)* with the liquid
¼ cup hoisin sauce*
Few drops red food color, optional
Honey to glaze

* Chinese ingredients may be found at Asian grocery stores or in the oriental section of most supermarkets.

Cranberry-Orange Bread

Jennie In bakes this bread every Christmas and has given away hundreds of loaves for past 50 years. She used to grease, flour, and bake her bread in empty walnut cans. Jennie would then cut the loaves into circular slices. The can-shaped quick breads wrap up nicely as gifts.

For a delicious breakfast, serve this tasty bread fresh from the oven with cream cheese or lightly toasted with butter. Yum!

YIELD: 6 MEDIUM LOAVES

6 cups flour
3 cups sugar
1 teaspoon salt
1½ tablespoons baking powder
1½ teaspoons baking soda
½ cup melted butter
Juice and zest of 3 oranges
Boiling water to make 2¼ cups liquid
3 eggs, beaten
2 cups raw cranberries, coarsely chopped
1½ cups chopped walnuts

Whisk together flour, sugar, salt, baking powder and baking soda in large bowl. Combine melted butter, juice and zest of 3 oranges; add enough boiling water to make 2¼ cups liquid. Make well in center of dry ingredients; add liquid ingredients all at once and mix well. Add beaten eggs, cranberries and nuts; mix together to blend well. Pour batter into 6 medium greased and floured loaf pans. Bake at 325°F until toothpick inserted in center of breads comes out clean, about 1 hour. Cool. Drizzle with icing or sprinkle with confectioner's sugar, if desired.

TIP: Bake in greased and floured empty cans for a novel look and size.

Date Nut Bread

YIELD: 1 9x5 LOAF

¼ cup butter, cut into 6 chunks

1 cup pitted dates, coarsely chopped

¼ cup brown sugar, packed

¼ cup granulated sugar

¾ cup boiling water

1 egg, beaten

2 cups flour

2 teaspoons baking powder

½ teaspoon salt

½ cup macadamia nut bits

½ teaspoon vanilla extract

1½ tablespoons rum, optional

An old recipe from my archives, this fruit bread makes an excellent hostess gift and travels well, especially when baked in miniature loaf pans. Fruit breads also freeze well, so bake when time allows so that you'll have something homemade time to serve your guests.

Place butter in large mixing bowl, add dates and both types of sugars. Pour boiling water over ingredients in the bowl; let stand 7 minutes. Stir well and let cool. When mixture is cool, add egg and mix well.

Sift together flour, baking powder and salt. Add to date mixture; beat 30 seconds. Stir in nuts, vanilla extract and rum, if used. Pour batter into a greased and floured loaf pan. Bake at 350°F for 45 to 50 minutes or until done.

Spicy Seasoned Hawaiian Salt

Simply basic best describes the flavors this seasoned salt imparts on steaks, chops, roasts, stews, soups and generally everything! Back to basics is a good thing!

YIELD: ABOUT 8 CUPS

5 pounds Hawaiian salt

⅓ cup coarse black pepper

⅓ cup minced garlic

⅓ cup grated fresh ginger

Crushed chili pepper to taste

Combine salt and pepper in large roasting pan; mix well. Add garlic and ginger using back of wooden spoon to mix well and mash pieces. Bake at 350°F for 25 to 30 minutes, stirring every 2 to 3 minutes, or until slightly brown and dry. Cool thoroughly. Store in covered jar in a cool place.

USE: Great on broiled or baked meats, fish, seafood and poultry. It is often used to flavor soups and stews.

Hawaiian Nut Bread

𝒫ineapple flourished in Hawai'i during the 20th century. Its exotic, sweet flavor and versatility for cooking delighted chefs and homemakers alike. It has become a widely-used ingredient in Island cooking. In this dish, the pineapple is complemented by the banana flavor. This quick bread can be served at breakfast or for dessert.

Grease or spray 9 x 5 x 3-inch loaf pan. Sift flour with baking powder, baking soda and salt. In separate bowl, combine pineapple, including liquid, bananas and orange juice. In large mixing bowl, cream butter and sugar until light and fluffy; add eggs, one at a time, beating well after each addition. Add flour mixture alternately with pineapple mixture, mixing only enough to moisten dry ingredients. Stir in nuts. Pour into prepared pan. Bake at 350°F for 60 to 75 minutes or until done.

YIELD: 1 9x5 LOAF

2 cups flour
2 teaspoons baking powder
1 teaspoon baking soda
½ teaspoon salt
1 can (8 ¼ oz.) crushed pineapple, including liquid
1 cup mashed bananas
¼ cup orange juice
½ cup butter
¾ cup sugar
2 eggs
2 cups macadamia nut bits

(Mutual Publishing)

Crispy Coconut Cookies

ookies make great gifts and tend to ship well. Crispy cookies, however, need to be packed very well to avoid crumbling. These cookies also make great hostess gifts.

YIELD: ABOUT 4 DOZEN

1 cup butter or margarine
1 cup sugar
1 ½ teaspoons vanilla extract
2 cups flour
1½ cups shredded coconut

In large mixing bowl, cream butter and sugar until light and fluffy. Add vanilla extract; beat thoroughly. Mix in flour; add coconut and mix well. Shape into walnut-size balls and place on ungreased baking sheets; flatten with bottom of a glass dipped in flour. Bake at 300°F for 20 to 25 minutes or until golden brown. Cool completely and store in airtight container at room temperature.

VARIATIONS:

CRISPY CHOCOLATE CHIP: Add 1 cup chocolate chip morsels to dough; omit shredded coconut.

CRISPY HAZELNUT: Add ¾ cup chopped hazelnuts after flour has been added; omit shredded coconut.

CRISPY LEMON: Add 2 tablespoons lemon zest after the flour has been added; omit shredded coconut.

CRISPY MACADAMIA NUT: Add ½ cup macadamia nut bits after flour has been added; omit shredded coconut.

CRISPY SPICY: Blend together 1½ teaspoons ground cinnamon, ½ teaspoon ground ginger and ¼ teaspoon nutmeg and add to mixture after flour has been added.

Dried Cranberry-Edamame Trail Mix

A wonderful, healthy, and delicious snack, this dish is made with dried, sweetened cranberries which are low cholesterol, fat free and a good source of fiber. Combined with dry-roasted edamame, this recipe is a great source of soy protein as well. Enjoy!

YIELD: 10 BAGS (7 OZ. EACH)

1 package (48 oz.) dried
   cranberries
1 container (29 oz.) dry roasted
   edamame (soy beans)

Combine dried cranberries and edamame in a large bowl; toss to mix well. Pack seven ounces of mix in zip-top plastic bags, sealable cellophane bags or clean jars with covers. Seal and store in cool place.

Spicy Oriental Corn Chips

Corn chips are great snacks that go especially well with dips. These chips, however, take that great taste to another level. The chips are flavored with a teriyaki-like sauce then sprinkled with furikake! You'll love them and once you start munching on these chips, you won't be able to stop.

YIELD: ABOUT 2½ QUARTS

Nonstick cooking spray
2 packages (13½ oz. each) bite-
   size corn chips
½ cup butter
½ cup sugar
½ cup light corn syrup
3 tablespoons soy sauce
¼ cup furikake (dried seaweed
   seasoning mx)
½ to 1 teaspoon hot sauce

Spray large, deep baking pan with cooking spray; add corn chips. In saucepan, heat butter with sugar, corn syrup, soy sauce and hot sauce; stir until sugar dissolves. Pour sauce over corn chips and sprinkle furikake over; toss lightly to combine. Bake, uncovered. Temperature: 250°F for 1 hour, mixing lightly every 15 minutes. After baking and while still hot, quickly separate any corn chips that are stuck together using 2 forks. Cool completely and store in airtight containers.

Mac Nut Butter Bars

Easy to make and easy to package and transport, these bars make great omiyage.

Grease a 13 x 9 x 2-inch pan; set aside. In large mixing bowl, cream butter and sugar together; beat in egg and vanilla extract. Mix in flour. Stir in ¾ cup of the nuts. Pour batter evenly into prepared pan; sprinkle with remaining nuts. Bake at 350°F for 25 to 30 minutes. While hot, cut into bars and remove from pan while still warm. Cool completely before packing or storing.

YIELD: 24 BARS

1 cup butter
1 cup sugar
1 egg
1 teaspoon vanilla extract
2 cups flour
1¼ cups macadamia nut bits

Dried Fruit Mui

During the Second World War "cracked seed" (preserved plum) was unavailable due to rationing. Island moms got creative by substituting the plum with other fruits. In my neighborhood as a girl, prune mui was popular because the fruit was easily found at the market.

In gallon-size plastic jar with lid, combine brown sugar, salt, whiskey, Chinese five-spice powder and lemon juice; mix well to combine. Add prunes and other dried fruits, lemon peel and li hing mui; cover and shake jar to coat fruits. Let stand for a minimum of 3 days at room temperature, mixing twice a day. Pack in plastic containers.

YIELD: 1 GALLON

1 pound dark brown sugar
3 tablespoons Hawaiian salt
3 tablespoons whiskey
1 tablespoon Chinese five-spice powder
2 cups fresh lemon juice
8 packages (12 oz. each) pitted prunes
2 packages (12 oz. each) dried apricots or mixed dried fruit
½ pound Chinese dried lemon peel, chopped
½ pound seedless li hing mui (dried plum)

Favorite Brownies

Brownies make a perfect omiyage. They are easy to make, package, and ship—and who doesn't like a good brownie? To make these even more decadent and delicious, add a layer of chocolate frosting.

Melt butter or margarine and chocolate in saucepan; remove from heat and stir in sugar. Mix together flour, salt and baking powder; add to chocolate mixture; beat in eggs then stir in nuts and vanilla extract. Pour into greased 9-inch square pan. Bake at 350°F for 25 minutes. Cool and cut into bars.

VARIATIONS:

CREAM CHEESE BROWNIES: Prepare Brownie as directed; set aside. Mix together 1 package (8 oz.) softened cream cheese, ⅓ cup sugar, 1 egg and ½ teaspoon vanilla extract; beat to blend thoroughly. Spread two-thirds of brownie batter in greased 8 or 9-inch pan. Spread cream cheese mixture evenly over batter. Spoon remaining brownie batter in heaps over cream cheese mixture. Using a knife or skewer; cut through batter several times for marble effect. Proceed as directed above.

CHOCOLATE CHIP BROWNIES: Add 1 cup chocolate chips to Favorite Brownie batter. Proceed as directed above

MAC NUT BROWNIES: Add 1 cup macadamia nut bits to Favorite Brownie batter. Proceed as directed above.

YIELD: ABOUT 16 PIECES

⅓ cup butter or margarine
1 square (1 oz.) unsweetened chocolate
1 cup sugar
¾ cup flour
½ teaspoon salt
½ teaspoon baking powder
2 eggs, slightly beaten
1 cup macadamia nut bits
1 teaspoon vanilla extract

For more recipes on omiyage from your kitchen, see Muriel Miura's books, Homemade Gifts of Sweets and Treats *and* Cookies from Hawai'i's Kitchen

Irish Soda Bread

A specialty of the Hilton Hawaiian Village Resort & Spa in Waikīkī, this tasty bread has been served with their banquet meal service for years. This recipe is shared with you just as it appeared in one of our local papers.

YIELD: 1 LOAF

1⅔ cups flour
3 tablespoons sugar
1 teaspoon baking powder
½ teaspoon baking soda
½ teaspoon salt
½ cup raisins or currants
2 teaspoons caraway seeds
1 large egg, beaten
¾ cup buttermilk
¼ cup unsalted butter, melted

Combine flour, sugar, baking powder, baking soda and salt in a large bowl; whisk together. Stir in raisins or currants and caraway seeds.

In a separate bowl, beat together buttermilk and butter. Add the liquid mixture to the dry mixture and stir just until dry ingredients are moistened. The batter will be stiff but sticky. Scrape batter onto baking sheet to form mound 6 to 7 inches in diameter or scrape into greased loaf pan; spread evenly. Using a sharp knife, slash large "X" about 1 to 2 inches deep into top of batter. Bake at 350°F for 25 to 30 minutes on baking sheet, or 45 to 60 minutes in loaf pan until golden brown and done.

Waikīkī, circa 1960s (Hawai'i State Archives)

Macadamia Nut Okoshi

Okoshi is a Japanese rice cracker and it is somewhat tricky to make. One must work quickly to fold in the puffed rice, otherwise the cracker will not be puffy nor crispy. Puffed brown rice can be substituted as a healthier alternative. Be prepared, however, to do some looking; puffed brown rice is not as common as the white variety.

Preheat oven to 200°F. Set out a large bowl, large rimmed cookie sheet and a spatula. Coat all three with cooking oil spray. Set out a small bowl of ice water. Spread cereal and macadamia nuts in a pan and place in oven to crisp for a few minutes.

Melt butter in saucepan over medium heat; add sugar, stirring continuously, until caramel color and thickened, about 5 to 10 minutes. Remove from heat.

Quickly remove cereal and macadamia nuts from oven and pour into greased bowl. Stir caramel sauce again then drizzle quickly over cereal mixture. Stir quickly with greased spatula to coat cereal; turn cereal mixture immediately onto greased cookie sheet and press mixture flat and even with buttered hands, or cover with waxed paper and press down until even. If mixture is too hot to touch, dip hands into ice water to cool and keep working. Cool slightly; cut into squares while warm.

TIP: Speed is of essence in making okoshi as the sauce hardens quickly and the cereal mixture will become difficult to handle. Cut into desired size while warm as it will become difficult to cut as it cools.

YIELD: 12-18 PIECES

5 cups puffed wheat or rice cereal
⅓ cup macadamia nut bits
¾ block butter
¾ cup sugar

Cocoa Mochi
(Cocoa Glutinous Rice Cake)

A common and tasty snack in Hawaiʻi, mochi is a gelatinous Japanese rice cake. There are numerous varieties of this Japanese rice cake available at markets in the Islands.

Grease 13 x 9 x 2-inch pan; set aside. In large mixing bowl, combine all ingredients and mix well. Pour into prepared 13 x 9-inch pan. Bake at 350°F for 1 hour. Cool before cutting.

YIELD: ABOUT 24 SERVINGS

2 cups mochiko (mochi rice flour)
1 can (12 oz.) frozen coconut milk, thawed
1¾ cups sugar
¼ cup butter, melted
3 tablespoons ground cocoa
Katakuriko (potato starch)
1 tablespoon baking soda
1 can (12 oz.) evaporated milk

Savory Pretzels

The sweetness of the pretzels and the saltiness from the dry ranch dressing mix and just a touch of furikake make these pretzels addicting. These pretzels make a great munchie while watching your favorite weekend game. Nothing can be easier to whip together in minutes!

Place pretzels in a re-sealable 2-gallon plastic bag. Add butter and seal bag; shake until evenly coated. Mix together Ranch Dressing mix, garlic powder and furikake in a small bowl. Add mixture to the bag; toss to coat pretzels evenly. Transfer to a cookie sheet to air-dry for about an hour. Store in air-tight containers.

YIELD: ABOUT 2½ QUARTS

3-4 packages (10 oz. each) pretzels
1 cup melted butter
1 package Ranch Dressing dry mix
2 tablespoons garlic powder
⅓ cup furikake
3 tablespoons dill, optional

Simply Sushi

Sushi, a Japanese dish of cold rice flavored with sweetened rice vinegar and shaped into small cakes, is very popular in Hawai'i and continues to grow in popularity. It is interesting to note that the origins of sushi are accidental. Centuries ago, fish was packed in rice as a way of preserving it. The rice fermented and this in turn preserved the fish. A variety of seafood, vegetables, and cooked meats are used in sushi dishes today.

Sushi counter, Evergreen Cafe, circa 1962
(Hawai'i State Archives)

Very little equipment is needed to make sushi. A special bamboo mixing tub (sushi–oke) would be useful, as would a pressing box (oshi waku) and a rice spatula (shamoji). Of course, a bamboo sushi mat (makisu or sudare) is a must and can be found in most Asian specialty stores.

Sushi comes in a wide variety of styles and shapes. Each family and region has its own favorite repertoire, many of which can be created in your own kitchen. Though it is impossible to cover the whole spectrum of sushi in a small section of this book, a few excellent examples appear below.

Just remember: the secret to good sushi is to prepare and utilize the freshest and finest ingredients with care and sensitivity to the balance of flavors.

Sushi Rice

inegar and sugar added to cooked short grain rice serves as a preservative as well as replicating the original taste of Sushi Rice from centuries ago when fish was packed in rice to preserve it, only to have the rice ferment and develop a unique, tangy flavor.

YIELD: 12 CUPS

4 cups short grain rice
4 cups water

VINEGAR SAUCE:

3¼ cups rice vinegar
⅓ cup salt
4 cups sugar
¼ cup mirin (sweet rice wine)

Wash rice and drain. Add water and let stand 20 to 30 minutes before cooking. Let water come to a boil; reduce heat to simmer and cook 5 to 8 minutes or until water level is reduced to level of rice. Cook additional 7 to 8 minutes over low heat. Let steam, covered, 10 minutes before transferring to large bowl or shallow wooden container.

Combine Vinegar Sauce ingredients. Cook over medium heat until sugar dissolves; cool. Sprinkle approximately 1 cup sauce over hot rice and toss gently using cutting strokes sideways with rice paddle to avoid mashing rice grains. Do not mix with circular motions. Add more Vinegar Sauce, if desired. Cool quickly using fan. Rice is now ready to make various types of sushi. Prepared Vinegar Sauce may be kept in a sealed bottle in the refrigerator for later use.

TIP: Use approximately 1 cup Vinegar Sauce to 5 cups cooked rice to make Sushi Rice.

Gunkan Zushi *(Sushi Boats)*

Sushi boats are made by wrapping nori (dried seaweed) around molded rice and toppings such as fish roe, minced tuna mixed with mayonnaise, or scallops. These boats are an attractive and tasty addition to any table.

Divide the rice into 8 batches. Shape each into an oval using moistened hand. Wrap a strip of nori around each oval mound of rice and trip off any excess, then join ends together at the join using a couple of crushed grains of rice. Dab a little wasabi paste on top of each sushi boat and top with tablespoon of desired topping. Serve with soy sauce on side.

TIP: Wasabi paste in a tube can be found at Asian grocers or in the oriental section of most supermarkets. Wasabi paste can be made by mixing wasabi powder with a little water to make a paste of desired consistency.

YIELD: ABOUT 8 PIECES

¾ cup Sushi Rice (see page 94)
2 small sheets toasted nori, each cut into 4 lengthwise strips
Wasabi paste
8 tablespoons desired topping

SUGGESTED TOPPINGS:

Tobiko (flying fish roe) or salmon roe
Smoked tuna or salmon mixed with mayonnaise
Minced fresh tuna and hot chili sauce mixed with mayonnaise
Crab and minced onion mixed with mayonnaise
Smoked salmon, thinly sliced, on rice and topped with thin slices cucumber and ginger

Maki Zushi *(Rolled Sushi)*

*R*olling maki-sushi is a popular and easy method of preparing sushi. Place a sheet of nori on a bamboo mat. Add to the nori a layer of Sushi Rice and fillings—the fillings can be any combination of vegetables, seafood, meats, poultry, even fruits, it's up to the cook—and roll the mat. Remove the bamboo mat and cut the roll into 7 to 8 pieces and serve with the cut side up to show the varied and colorful interior.

Maki-sushi can be made thin (hoso-maki) or fat (futo-maki) and may be served with soy sauce, mayonnaise or sweet chili sauce. It is usually accompanied by a mound of sweet pickled ginger and wasabi.

During World War II when nori was not available in Hawai'i, creative local homemakers substituted large, blanched napa cabbage leaves for nori. You, too, may find some other vegetables that can be used to substitute nori.

YIELD: ABOUT 6-8 ROLLS

12 cups Sushi Rice
(see page 94)
9 sheets nori (laver), 9 fried
egg sheets or 9 large
blanched napa cabbage
leaves
Mayonnaise, optional
Wasabi paste, optional

SUGGESTED FILLINGS:

Watercress, blanched
Cooked carrots, cut in lengthwise
strips
Smoke salmon fillet, cut in batons
Asparagus spears, cooked
Cucumbers, cut in lengthwise strips
Ripe avocados, cut in lengthwise
strips
Kaiware (radish sprouts), washed
and drained

Takuwan (pickled radish), cut in
lengthwise strips
Imitation crab sticks, cut into
lengthwise batons or logs
Fresh fillet of tuna, cut in 3-inch strips
or batons
Unagi (seasoned cooked eel), cut in
strips
Teriyaki chicken, cooked and cut in
strips
Pork Cutlet, cooked and cut in strips
Smoked salmon

Place 1 sheet of nori, shiny side down, on bamboo mat. Using wet hands, spread 1½ to 2 cups Sushi Rice evenly over three-quarters of the nori sheet leaving about 1-inch margin on end farthest from you. Spread a small amount of wasabi paste onto the rice at the end nearest you then spread on the mayonnaise (if using wasabi and mayonnaise). Layer 5 to 7 vegetable and fish fillings on rice.

To roll the sushi, fold mat over, starting at the end nearest you where the fillings are and tuck in the end of the nori to start the roll. Roll like for jelly roll, lifting up the mat as you go and keeping the pressure evenly but gently until filling is completely encased. Press mat gently, but firmly, around roll to shape and tighten sushi. Remove mat and let rest before cutting. Cut each roll into 7 or 8 pieces with sharp, moistened knife. Arrange on platter, cut side up, garnish with mounds of beni-shoga (sweet pickled ginger) and soy sauce to serve.

VARIATIONS:
Blanched napa cabbage or fried egg sheet may be substituted for nori.

Uramaki Zushi
(Inside Out Rolled Sushi)

Follow the recipe for Maki Zushi except, the Uramaki Zushi directions are different as noted below.

Line sushi mat with plastic wrap, overlap in back of mat and secure with tape. Place a sheet of nori, shiny-side down, on plastic covered side of mat. With wet hands, spread 1½-2 cup Sushi Rice in an even layer on the nori, pressing down gently. Arrange desired amount of fillings from above list on top of the rice about 1½-inches from the edge nearest you. Roll like you would jelly roll, lifting up the mat as you go and keep the pressure even but gently until fill is completely encased. Press firmly. Remove mat and roll sushi in pan sprinkled with toasted sesame seeds. Place seam side down on waxed paper; let rest before slicing into 7 to 8 slices with sharp, moistened knife. Arrange on platter, cut side up, garnish with mounds of beni-shoga and soy sauce to serve.

Oshi Zushi (Pressed/Molded Sushi)

*O*ne of the easiest types of sushi to make, pressed and box sushi (Oshi Zushi and hako-zushi) is made using a three-piece mold (oshi waku) (though a pan with a loose bottom or a terrine mold with sides that drop down may serve as a substitute). If using a fixed base pan, the sushi toppings are placed in the pan first and Sushi Rice is placed on top of the toppings then pressed down. The sushi is inverted and cut as desired. Garnish with pickled ginger and serve with soy sauce-wasabi sauce.

California Oshi Zushi
(California Pressed/Molded Sushi)

A variation of the California Roll, this sushi uses the same ingredients except the filling ingredients are placed on top of the Sushi Rice in a 2 or 3-piece mold instead of rolled. Rolled or pressed, however, this sushi tastes great!

Oil or moisten Japanese sushi mold or 8-inch loose-bottom square cake pan and line with plastic wrap so that the plastic hangs over the edges. Pack the mold with Sushi Rice. Spread layer of mayonnaise on top of the rice then sprinkle over with sesame seeds. Artistically arrange avocado, crab and cucumber on top of rice; cover and press down. Chill 10 to 15 minutes. Remove from mold; sprinkle with nori strips. Cut as desired with sharp, wet knife. Serve with pickled ginger and wasabi paste.

YIELD: 4 SERVINGS

6 cups Sushi Rice (see page 94)
3 tablespoons mayonnaise
1 teaspoon toasted sesame
   seeds
⅓ avocado, cut into strips
4 crab sticks, diagonally sliced
½ Japanese cucumber, thinly
   sliced diagonally
½ cup toasted nori strips

Layered Sushi

*L*ayered sushi is Hawai'i's contribution to the sushi tradition. This type of sushi is made simply by alternately layering Sushi Rice with fillings in a square or rectangular pan. It is easy to make and feeds many, making it a perfect addition to any tailgate party, family gathering, or party.

YIELD: ABOUT 24 PIECES

12 cups Sushi Rice
(see page 94)

TOPPINGS:

2 cans tuna, drained
2 tablespoons mirin
¼ cup sugar
¼ cup soy sauce
Red or green oboro (shrimp flakes)
Thin fried egg strips
Beni-shoga (pickled red ginger),
optional
1 package (1.4 oz.) shiofuke konbu
(beef steak plant flavored
seasoning)

Stir-fry tuna, mirin, sugar and soy sauce in non-stick skillet 1 to 2 minutes over medium heat, stirring constantly. Cool.

Line 9 x 13-inch pan with waxed paper. Sprinkle shrimp flakes evenly in pan. Sprinkle with egg strips, then with seasoned tuna. Top with Sushi Rice. Cover with waxed paper and press down firmly. Cool completely. Invert on to serving tray; cut into desired pieces. Garnish with beni-shoga, if desired.

VARIATION: Divide Sushi Rice into two portions; spread only one portion rice over tuna then sprinkle 1 package (1.4 oz.) shiofuke konbu over rice. Spread remaining portion of Sushi Rice over konbu. Cover rice with waxed paper; press down firmly. Cool completely then cut into desired pieces.

Inari Zushi
(Cone Sushi/Rice Filled Tofu Pouches)

Inari, or cone sushi as it is called in Hawai'i, are the little tofu pouches, seasoned with sugar and soy sauce, filled with Sushi Rice. Cone sushi is a favorite quick snack here in the Islands. Flavored tofu pouches are available in most Asian markets which makes this type of sushi ever so easy to prepare.

FILLING: Combine all ingredients for Sushi Rice Filling in large bowl; toss gently to mix well. Set aside.

ABURA-AGE: To prepare the cone, cut abura-age in half, crosswise, and place in colander. Pour boiling water over; drain and set aside. Combine mirin, sake, sugar, soy sauce and water in medium saucepan and cook over medium heat until sugar dissolves. Add abura-age and simmer, uncovered, over low heat until all the liquid is absorbed; cool and stuff with Sushi Rice Filling. Do not stuff too tightly. To serve, arrange sushi side up; garnish with beni shoga (pickled red ginger), if desired.

YIELD: ABOUT 24 PIECES

SUSHI RICE FILLING:

4 cups Sushi Rice (see page 94)
2 tablespoons toasted sesame seeds
½ cup slivered carrot, cooked
¼ cup minced string beans or peas, cooked

ABURA-AGE (TOFU POUCHES)* :

12 abura-age (fried tofu pouches)
2 tablespoons mirin (sweet rice wine)
3 tablespoons sake (rice wine)
¼ cup sugar
¼ cup soy sauce
1½ cups water

* Seasoned tofu pouches are available at most Asian markets and in the oriental section of some supermarkets.

Chirashi Zushi *(Scattered Sushi)*

Chirashi Zushi, or scattered sushi, is easy to make, but presentation is essential. Sushi Rice is placed in a beautiful individual serving bowl. Colorful, fresh toppings are arranged atop the rice. Any ingredients and toppings may be uses as long as the result is colorful and appetizing. Pickled ginger and wasabi are added as garnish or served separately in little dishes alongside the soy sauce and mayonnaise for dipping.

Nigiri Zushi *(Hand Molded Sushi)*

Originally developed in Tokyo as street finger food, nigiri zushi is prepared with a selection of the freshest seafood. Sushi Rice is molded into small oval shapes and topped with a touch of wasabi paste under slices of fresh raw fish, calamari, prawn or scallops. It is dipped in soy sauce and eaten within minutes of making.

Bring water and salt to boil in saucepan over high heat. Add shrimp and calamari; cook 1 minute. Drain. Shell, clean and cut shrimp in lengthwise halves. In small dish, mix few drops water with wasabi; mix well and set aside.

For each sushi, press about 2-3 tablespoons Sushi Rice into an oval mound, about 2 x 1 x 1-inch in size. Dab a pinch of wasabi paste on one side of the rice mount; top with shrimp, fish or calamari slice. Serve with soy sauce-wasabi mixture to dip.

YIELD: ABOUT 24 SUSHI

1 cup water
½ teaspoon salt
4 large shrimp
8 slices calamari
1 ¼ teaspoon wasabi
4 cups Sushi Rice (see page 94)
8 slices fresh raw fish (tuna, sea bass, hamachi, marlin)

Temaki Zushi *(Hand Rolled Sushi)*

Sushi Rice is hand rolled in seasoned nori (seaweed laver) with filling ingredients of the diner's choice. The Temaki Sushi may be served with soy sauce as dip.

'Ahi Tataki Temaki
(Hand Rolled Tuna Sushi)

YIELD: 6 PIECES

1 teaspoon fresh ground black pepper
1 tablespoon grated fresh ginger
1 tablespoon toasted sesame seeds
8 ounces very fresh tuna fillet
Salt to taste
2 tablespoons canola oil
3 large sheets toasted nori, halved
1½ cups Sushi Rice (see page 94)
½ small Japanese cucumber, cut into lengthwise strips or baton
¼ cup mayonnaise
Wasabi paste

Mix together pepper, ginger and sesame seeds in small bowl; rub mixture into all sides of fish fillet, pressing sesame seeds on firmly. Season tuna lightly with salt. Heat oil in skillet then sear tuna on all sides for 2 to 3 minutes or until surface turns white but center portion remains uncooked. Remove from skillet and cool. Slice fish into thin slices.

Place piece of nori in palm of hand and spread about 3 tablespoons Sushi Rice evenly on nori to cover bottom two-thirds of the nori. Dab a little wasabi paste along the center of the rice and lay tuna and cucumber on the rice, then drizzle over with a little mayonnaise.

Wrap nori around filling, starting at lower end of nori and rolling into cone shape. Paste the join together with a couple of crushed grains of rice. Repeat with remaining pieces of nori. Dip in soy sauce to eat.

E Pā'ina Kākou...
Let's Party!

It's hard to imagine a more dramatic setting than smack in the middle of the Pacific on an island basking in the tropical sunshine under blue skies. Having a get-together with a dozen or more friends in Hawai'i means "casual and relaxed." It is all about having fun with less demanding food.

It is all about that unforgettable spaghetti with Bolognese sauce that you made well ahead and need only a salad to complete the meal… which means, you have lots of time to sit back and enjoy the company. This chapter makes entertaining easier for you! E Pā'ina Kākou!

(Mutual Publishing)

Saucy Ribs

Ribs are easy to prepare and require very little attention while cooking. Serve these ribs with your favorite baked beans and a nice tossed salad.

Prepare sauce of choice and use as directed in chart below. Cut ribs into pieces to fit aluminum foil-lined pan. Place meat sides up on rack in pan. Cook as directed at 325°F.

YIELD: ABOUT 6 SERVINGS

4½ pounds pork loin back ribs, pork spareribs or beef ribs
3 pounds pork country-style ribs
Spicy Barbecue Sauce or Mustard Sauce

SPICY BARBECUE SAUCE:

1 large onion, chopped
2 cups catsup
⅓ Worcestershire sauce
¼ cup brown sugar, packed
2 tablespoons prepared mustard
1 tablespoon chili powder
2 teaspoons liquid smoke
2 teaspoons salt

MUSTARD SAUCE:

½ cup molasses
⅓ cup Dijon mustard
⅓ cup cider vinegar

SPICY BARBECUE SAUCE: Combine all sauce ingredients in saucepan; cover and cook over low heat for 5 minutes, stirring frequently; brush on ribs.

MUSTARD SAUCE: Mix together molasses and mustard; stir in vinegar; brush on ribs.

COOKING CHART		
Kind of Ribs	**Pan**	**Cooking Directions**
Pork: Loin or Back Ribs	Rack in shallow roasting pan	Bake uncovered 1½ hours; brush with sauce. Bake uncovered 45 minutes longer; brush with sauce often until tender.
Pork: Spareribs	Rack in shallow roasting pan	Bake uncovered 1 hour; brush with sauce, bake uncovered 30 minutes longer, brush with sauce often until tender
Pork: Country-style Ribs	13 x 9 x 2 inch pan	Cover and bake 2 hours or until tender; drain. Pour sauce over ribs. Bake uncovered 30 minutes longer.

Baked Hoisin Barbecue Ribs

These pork ribs are flavored with hoisin—a spicy, salty-sweet brown sauce made of soybeans, sugar, garlic, Chinese five-spice powder, chile and red rice for coloring—and glazed with a layer of delicious honey.

Remove excess fat and tissues from ribs. Brush hoisin sauce on both sides and let stand in refrigerator overnight. Place pork ribs on rack on foil-lined baking pans. Brush with additional hoisin sauce on one side. Bake at 350°F for 30 minutes. Turn, brush with sauce on other side and bake additional 30 minutes or until done. Brush honey on both sides and leave in oven additional 5 minutes to glaze. Remove from oven; let stand 5 minutes before separating ribs; cut into desired sizes to serve.

YIELD: 6-8 SERVINGS

2 racks of pork ribs
1 jar (15 oz.) hoisin sauce
1 jar (12 oz.) honey

Sweet Sour Spareribs

...vorite recipe given to me by a dear friend ...s a student at the University of Hawaiʻi. ...pork variation of this dish, one inch ...t may be substituted.

...stick pot over medium-high heat, ...ger and garlic. Stir in water, brown ...cover and bring to a boil. Lower ...0 minutes or until tender. ...pples with liquid; stir and ...dd cornstarch slurry; ...ned rice.

YIELD: 10-12 SERVINGS

6 pounds spareribs, cut into 1½-inch pieces
1 small onion, coarsely chopped
1 small piece fresh ginger, sliced and crushed
1 clove garlic, crushed
1 cup water
1 cup brown sugar, packed
¾ cup white vinegar
¼ cup soy sauce
1 teaspoon salt
1 can (28 oz.) pineapple chunks, undrained
3 tablespoons cornstarch mixed with 3 tablespoons water to make a slurry

Roast Pork with Rosemary

ork is a versatile meat and can be served with anything, anytime of the week. Still, you'll want to change things up once in a while. This dish of rosemary infused pork roast adds wonderful flavor to an already tasty ingredient!

YIELD: ABOUT 12 SERVINGS

3-4 pound pork loin or Boston butt roast
2 tablespoons chopped fresh rosemary
4 cloves garlic, minced
1 teaspoon salt
½ teaspoon pepper
1 tablespoon margarine or butter
¼ cup chopped onion
2 tablespoons canola oil

Trim fat from pork roast. Mix rosemary and garlic. Make 8 to 10 deep slits about 2-inches apart in pork with sharp knife; insert small amounts of garlic mixture into slits. Sprinkle pork with salt and pepper.

Melt margarine or butter in shallow roasting pan in oven; sprinkle with onion. Place pork on rack in roasting pan; drizzle with canola oil. Insert meat thermometer so that tip is in center of thickest part of pork but does not touch fat. Roast, uncovered at 350° F for 1¾ to 2 hours or until thermometer reads 160°F. Let stand 15 minutes before slicing. Serve with gravy using your favorite recipe.

Shabu Shabu Nabe
(Japanese-Style One Pot Dish)

The name of the dish, shabu shabu, comes from the swishing sound made as the ingredients are being cooked in the hot broth. The dish originated in Northern China or Mongolia and was adopted by the Japanese about a century ago.

For this interactive dinner, a brass hook nabe, sometimes called a "Mongolian hot pot," is used but a heavy skillet or casserole atop a camping or induction burner at the table serves just as well. As the broth cooks the meat and vegetables, it becomes a flavorful homemade soup.

YIELD: 4 SERVINGS

2 pounds top sirloin, cut into paper thin slices

6 cups chicken or beef broth

½ block tofu, cubed

1 bunch watercress, cut in 1½ inch lengths

8-10 napa cabbage leaves, cut in 1½-inch lengths

4 fresh shiitake mushrooms, cleaned and stems removed

1 medium round onion, thinly sliced

12 stems green onion, cut in 1½-inch lengths

½ pound broccoli spears, cut in 1½-inch lengths

½ pound cooked udon (thick Japanese noodles)

Arrange beef, vegetables and noodles on platter and place on dining table. Combine ingredients for Ponzu and pour into four small dishes and set before diners. Each guest cooks a choice of beef, tofu or vegetables in the boiling broth.

Bring broth to a boil; dip beef in the boiling broth until it turns pink. Cook tofu and vegetables in the hot broth until of desired doneness. Add the noodles last and cook only until reheated; serve with broth, if desired. Dip cooked ingredients in Ponzu or Goma Ae before eating. Serve with hot steamed rice.

TO MAKE PONZU: Combine ingredients; mix well.

TO MAKE GOMA AE: Combine all ingredients in blender; puree until smooth.

VARIATION: Boneless chicken or seafood may be added or substituted for beef.

TIP: The broth may be served as the last course, if desired.

PONZU (SOY-VINEGAR SAUCE):

1 cup soy sauce
¼ cup rice vinegar
¼ teaspoon hot chili sauce

GOMA AE (SESAME DIP)

⅓ cup toasted sesame seeds
¼ cup water
2 tablespoons soy sauce
1 tablespoon rice vinegar
1 teaspoon sesame oil
1 teaspoon peanut butter, optional
½ teaspoon minced fresh ginger
½ teaspoon sugar
⅛ teaspoon hot red pepper flakes

Roast Beef

This delicious recipe for roast beef never fails to please. It's also perfect for those cooks on the go: simply place the roast in the oven for half an hour before heading out of the house in the morning (be sure to turn the oven off before leaving); upon returning, just turn the oven on 30 minutes before dinner and voilà!, dinner is served.

Leave roast out of refrigerator and let stand at room temperature about 2 hours. Salt and pepper to taste; place on rack in shallow roasting plan lined with aluminum foil for easy cleaning. Roast at 400°F for 60 minutes. Turn oven off and leave roast in oven to rest minimum of 3 hours. DO NOT OPEN OVEN DOOR. 20 minutes before serving, turn oven on at 300°F and roast for 20 minutes. Serve with au jus or gravy of your choice.

TIP: If using packaged au jus or gravy mix, follow package directions.

YIELD: SERVING SIZE VARIES

Beef rib or cross rib roast, any size (allow 4-6 oz. cooked portion/person)
Hawaiian salt to taste
Freshly ground pepper to taste

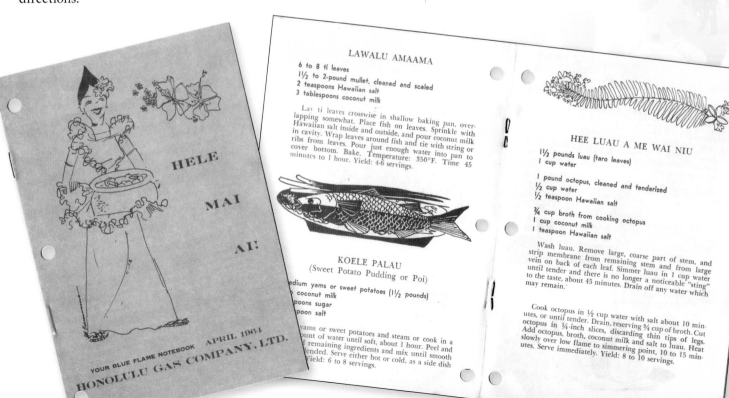

Burgundy Braised Short Ribs
3660 on the Rise

YIELD: 6 SERVINGS

½ cup oil

6 each, 3-bone short ribs,
2-inch thick (cut between
bone)

½ cup small diced bacon

1 tablespoon minced shallots

5 cloves garlic, peeled

1 teaspoon fresh Thyme

½ teaspoon Rosemary

3 cups burgundy wine

3 quarts beef broth or stock

1 cup small diced carrots

1 cup small diced onions

3 cups mushrooms, quartered

½ cup caramel sauce

1½ cups pearl onions

¾ cup unsalted butter

¾ cup flour

Salt and pepper to taste

Burgundy Braised Short Ribs is one of Executive Chef Russell Siu's popular dishes at Honolulu restaurant 3660 on the Rise. The recipe is delicious, the presentation is beautiful, and the preparation is simple, too—especially since Chef Siu has been gracious enough to share his recipe below!

In a brazier add oil and short ribs. Brown over medium high heat until ribs are nice and brown. Add bacon, shallots, garlic, thyme, rosemary and mix. Simmer for about 4 minutes; add burgundy wine. Simmer another 4 minutes and then add beef stock, carrots and onions. Cover and simmer for about 1½ hours over low heat. Add mushrooms and simmer until short ribs are tender. Add caramel and pearl onions; simmer for about 6 minutes. Mix together butter and flour until smooth; add slowly to short ribs, stirring constantly, for about 15 minutes. Season with salt and pepper.

Hawaiian Beef Curry Stew

This full-bodied curry stew is so good, it will attract a crowd. Bits of beef are slow-cooked until juicy and tender, and crisp vegetables are added to give the dish some texture, taste, and color.

Dredge meat in flour; brown meat in hot oil. Add garlic, onion, salt and pepper; stir. Add 2½ quarts water; cover and simmer for 1½ to 2 hours or until meat is tender. Add celery, carrots and potatoes; cover and simmer 20 to 30 minutes. Mix curry powder and flour with water and slowly stir into stew; cook, stirring constantly, until mixture thickens. Adjust seasoning as necessary.

YIELD: ABOUT 12 SERVINGS

2½ pounds chuck or stew meat
¾ cup flour
2 tablespoons canola oil
1 clove garlic, minced
2 medium onions, wedged
2 teaspoons salt
¼ teaspoon pepper
2 ½ quarts water
2 ribs celery, sliced diagonally
4 carrots, pared and cut into
    1-inch pieces
4 potatoes, pared and cut into
    1-inch pieces
2 tablespoons curry powder or
    more, if desired
½ cup flour
1 cup water

(Mutual Publishing)

Gun Goki
(Korean-Style Barbecued Beef)

*K*orean cuisine is sometimes similar to that of the Japanese. This dish, for instance, is very similar to teriyaki beef. However, as is typical in Korean cooking, sesame oil and seeds are used to give the steak an added bit of flavor. Along with galbi (barbecued short ribs), Gun Goki is very popular among locals.

YIELD: ABOUT 8 SERVINGS

3 pounds flank steak

MARINADE:

⅓ cup toasted sesame seeds
⅓ cup salad oil
2 teaspoons sesame oil
½ cup soy sauce
¼ cup sugar
⅔ cup chopped onion
½ cup minced green onion
2 cloves garlic, crushed
2 slices fresh ginger, slivered
½ teaspoon pepper

Remove tendon and trim steak. Pound and score; cut into 3 x 4-inch pieces. Combine all Marinade ingredients in bowl; mix well and spread on beef pieces. Marinate minimum of 1 hour. Place on cold broiler pan; broil or grill 3 to 4 minutes on each side or until of desired doneness. Serve hot with steamed rice.

VARIATIONS:

GALBI (BARBECUED SHORT RIBS): Marinate scored beef short ribs in above marinade 1 hour or longer. Proceed as directed above.

KOREAN STYLE BARBECUED PORK: Substitute lean pork tenderloin for beef. Proceed as directed above.

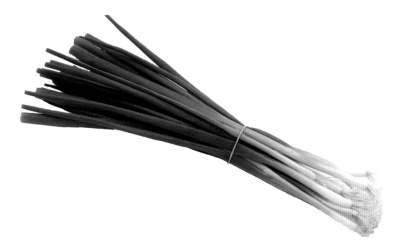

Oven Pot Roast

When entertaining, a dish that doesn't require much attention is welcome as it allows the hosts time to attend to guests and conversation. This Oven Pot Roast is just such a dish. Once in the oven, it requires little attention and the clean up is easy.

Trim fat from roast; place on large piece of heavy duty aluminum foil in roasting pan. Mix water and dry onion soup mix in bowl; pour over meat. Bring ends of foil over meat and seal. Roast at 350°F for 2 hours. Open foil carefully; add vegetables. Cook additional 30 to 45 minutes or until vegetables are done and meat is tender.

YIELD: ABOUT 8 SERVINGS

4 pounds pot roast (chuck, round or rump)
¾ cup water
1 package (1¾ oz.) dry onion soup mix
4 medium carrots, cut in 1-inch pieces
4 medium potatoes, quartered
1 cup celery, cut in ½-inch pieces
1 large onion, wedged

Herb Leg of Lamb

Lamb is a delicate, flavorful meat and it requires spices that will accent its wonderful taste. This recipe employs garlic, rosemary, marjoram and thyme—seasonings that complement the lamb wonderfully.

Place leg of lamb, fat side up, on rack in an open baking pan. Combine garlic, salt and pepper with olive oil; spread over lamb. Mix herbs and flour; sprinkle over lamb. Combine wine and water; pour slowly over lamb. Roast at 300°F for 30 to 35 minutes per pound, or until meat thermometer registers 180°F. Serve with mint jelly, your favorite gravy or au jus.

YIELD: 8-10 SERVINGS

1 leg of lamb (about 6 ½ lbs.)
2 cloves garlic, crushed
1 teaspoon salt
Dash of coarse ground pepper
2 tablespoons extra virgin olive oil
1 teaspoon marjoram
1 teaspoon thyme
1 teaspoon rosemary
2 tablespoons flour
1 cup white wine
½ cup water

Roasted Lemon Soy Chicken

A recipe from one of my dearest friends, this dish puts a new spin on the traditional roasted chicken by infusing it with the zesty and clean flavors of ginger and lemon.

YIELD: 4-6 SERVINGS

1 (3-4 lbs.) chicken, cleaned and dried

MARINADE:

½ cup canola oil
⅓ cup fresh lemon juice
¼ cup soy sauce
1 clove garlic, minced
¾ teaspoon grated fresh ginger
½ teaspoon salt
¼ teaspoon pepper

Mix together all Marinade ingredients in bowl; Coat chicken with Marinade. Cover and refrigerate 4 hours or overnight. Drain and place chicken on rack in foil lined roasting pan. Bake at 325°F for 1 hour or until meat thermometer inserted in thigh registers 170°F. Brush chicken occasionally while roasting. After removing from oven, let rest 20 minutes before serving.

TIP: If desired, reserve pan juices in roasting pan. Add ½ cup chicken broth, 2 tablespoons lemon juice and 1 teaspoon soy sauce; whisk, stirring to loosen brown bits. Simmer until slightly thickened. Adjust seasoning as necessary. Serve with chicken.

Chinese-Style Roast Duck

he combination of several Asian flavors creates a pleasing taste and texture for this roasted duck. The juicy slices of the roasted duck can even be paired with crisp, crunchy vegetables as filling for a Southeast Asian-type summer roll using the rice paper wrapper. This dish is often served at Chinese banquets.

YIELD: ABOUT 6 SERVINGS

4-5 pound duck, cleaned and rinsed

MARINADE:

⅓ cup soy sauce
2 tablespoons dark bean sauce
1 teaspoon ground cinnamon
¼ cup green onion, cut in 1½-inch lengths
2 tablespoons dark brown sugar
2 cloves garlic, minced
½ teaspoon Chinese five-spices

BASTING SAUCE:

¼ cup soy sauce
1 tablespoon sugar
1 clove garlic, minced
½ teaspoon minced fresh ginger

Tie neck to close duck cavity. Combine all ingredients for Marinade; mix well and pour into body cavity of duck. Insert skewers across opening and lace tightly with string to prevent sauce from running out. Place duck, breast side up, on rack in shallow roasting pan filled with about 1 inch of water.

Combine ingredients for Basting Sauce and brush generously over duck. Let stand 45 minutes before cooking. Roast at 325°F for 1 hour or until duck is done. Baste occasionally with basting sauce during roasting. Serve with hoisin or plum sauce.

Birthday celebration, Lau Yee Chai, circa 1952 (Bishop Museum)

Coq Au Vin *(Braised Chicken)*

Celery adds an intriguing earthiness to this easy braised chicken recipe, while the white wine and garlic infuse it with richness.

Pat chicken pieces dry and season with salt and pepper. Sear chicken, skin side down, in hot oil in large skillet over medium-high heat until golden brown (do not turn), 3 to 5 minutes; transfer to plate. Pour off all but 2 tablespoons fat from skillet. Stir-fry garlic and celery in skillet over medium heat until golden and just beginning to soften, about 3 to 4 minutes. Add wine and bring to a boil, uncovered, until reduced by about half, about 2 to 3 minutes. Add water and bring to a boil. Return chicken, skin side up, to skillet and simmer over low heat, partially covered, for 25 to 30 minutes or until cooked through. Sprinkle with parsley to serve.

YIELD: 4 TO 6 SERVINGS

2 pounds (6 pieces) chicken thighs with skin and bone
1 teaspoon salt
¼ teaspoon pepper
2 tablespoons olive oil
4 cloves garlic, halved
3 celery ribs, cut into 1-inch pieces
1 cup dry white wine
1 cup water
2 tablespoons minced flat-leaf parsley

Oven Fried Chicken

*F*ried Chicken is a quintessential American dish. It's widely beloved and featured on dining tables across the land. What's not so beloved, however, is the oil and grease the chicken is fried in (especially in these times of calorie-counting consciousness). Here is an "oven fried" recipe that cuts out the grease and is just as delicious!

YIELD: 10 TO 12 SERVINGS

1½ cups buttermilk
1 teaspoon salt
½ teaspoon freshly ground black pepper
5 pounds chicken thighs, rinsed and dried
1½ cups bread crumbs
½ cup flour
2 teaspoons salt
2 teaspoons paprika
¼ teaspoon pepper
¼ cup macadamia nut bits, optional
2-3 cups mayonnaise

Mix together buttermilk, salt and ½ teaspoon pepper in large bowl; marinate chicken pieces overnight in refrigerator. In another bowl, mix together bread crumbs, flour, salt, paprika, pepper and macadamia nuts, if used; set aside. Remove chicken from buttermilk marinade and allow to "dry" in refrigerator for about 1 hour. Roll chicken pieces in mayonnaise then dredge in bread crumb mixture being careful to coat all sides of chicken. Place chicken, skin side down, on shallow oil sprayed foil-lined baking pan.

Bake at 350°F for 30 minutes. Turn and bake 30 additional minutes or until tender and done.

Yaki Zakana
(Broiled Fish)

Mochizuki Tea House in Liliha, circa 1950 (Bishop Museum)

Broiling or baking whole fish in the oven is a popular Japanese method of cooking fish at steakhouses—it is simple, healthy, and fast. This preparation method can also be applied to fish fillets or steaks as well.

Cut slits into both sides of fish; sprinkle with salt to taste; let stand 30 minutes. Rinse salt off and pat dry with absorbent paper. If desired, sprinkle surface of fish lightly with salt; wrap tail in foil to prevent burning. Place fish on broiler or baking pan covered with foil. Broil 5-8 minutes on each side, or until done. Spread surface of fish with mayonnaise and return to broiler. Broil additional 30 seconds or until mayonnaise begins to bubble. Garnish with green onion, ginger root, or paprika before serving, if desired.

VARIATIONS: Tai (bream) may be substituted for ʻōpakapaka.

TIP: Time required for broiling and baking fish will differ depending on weight and size of fillets and whole fish. Allow about 6-ounce serving per person for whole fish; 4-ounce serving for steaks and fillets.

YIELD: ABOUT 4 SERVINGS

1 whole (2-3 lbs.) ʻōpakapaka
  (gray snapper), scaled and
  cleaned
Salt to taste
Mayonnaise to taste
4 stalks green onion or ginger
  root, optional
Paprika, optional

Green Tea Noodle Shrimp Tempura

This delicate recipe consists of subtly flavored green tea noodles wrapped around tender shrimp. The shrimp are then dipped in a chilled batter and fried until light and crispy. This dish is best eaten while still hot.

YIELD: 10 SHRIMP TEMPURA

2 ounces green tea soba
   noodles
Ice water
½ cup flour
1 egg yolk
⅓ cup water
⅓ cup ice cubes (flakes
   preferred)
10 large fresh shrimp with tails
   on, peeled and deveined
1 tablespoon cornstarch
Canola oil for deep frying

DIPPING SAUCE:

1 cup water
1 package dashi-no-moto
¼ cup mirin (sweet rice wine)
¼ cup soy sauce
1½ tablespoons sugar

Cook soba noodles for 5 to 7 minutes in rapidly boiling water until al dente, about 5 minutes. Drain then plunge in ice water to cool. Drain and set aside.

Combine flour, egg yolk and ⅓ cup water in mixing bowl; whisk until smooth. Add ice cubes and whisk until well-blended. Lightly coat shrimp with cornstarch. Dip a few (2 to 3) strands of noodles in the batter; remove and wrap shrimp in coated noodles. Repeat with remaining shrimp. Gently lower noodle-wrapped shrimp, a few at a time, in oil heated to 365° to 375°F. Deep-fry 1 to 2 minutes or until light golden brown. Drain on absorbent paper. Serve hot with Dipping Sauce.

TO PREPARE DIPPING SAUCE: Combine all ingredients in saucepan and bring to a boil. Cool. If desired, ½ cup grated daikon (white radish) and 1 tablespoon minced green onion may be added as condiments before serving.

NOTE: Japanese green tea soba noodles (Cha Soba) are sold in packets at Asian grocery stores or in the oriental sections of some supermarkets. Regular, unflavored soba (buckwheat) noodles may also be used.

Fried Curried Mahimahi

*O*nce, years ago, I was hosting a dinner for several very important out of town guests. I felt that it was imperative that I serve them something that represented Hawai'i. After testing numerous dishes, I decided upon this recipe for mahimahi, with its exotic combination of flavors. It turned out to be a winner!

Combine marinade ingredients; mix well and marinate fish fillets 30 minutes. Dip fish in egg and dredge in panko. Deep fry in oil heated to 365°F. until golden brown on both sides, about 3 minutes. Drain on absorbent paper. Serve hot.

YIELD: 4 SERVINGS

1 pound mahimahi fillet, cut into serving slices and scored
1 egg, beaten
1 cup panko (Japanese flour meal)
1 quart salad oil for frying

MARINADE:

1 tablespoon sugar
1 teaspoon salt
1 tablespoon mirin (sweet rice wine)
2 teaspoons curry powder
2 tablespoons cornstarch
1 tablespoon soy sauce

50th State Favorites

YOUR BLUE FLAME NOTEBOOK – OCTOBER 1960

HONOLULU GAS COMPANY

TROPICAL PINEAPPLE PIE

Shell:
ce cans coconut flakes
ons butter, melted
oconut flakes in butter on thermostatically
p burner set at 300°F., stirring constantly.
cup of browned coconut for topping. Press
xture on bottom and sides of 10-inch pie

eapple tidbits and syrup
n juice

edients and cook on thermo-
rner at 250°F. until mixture
ve from flame and stir in
l until mixture is slightly
s, water and dry milk and
mixture into chilled pine-
t shell. Sprinkle top with
n GAS refrigerator until

BANANA TEA MUFFINS

1 egg
1/3 cup salad oil
1/2 cup sugar
1 cup mashed bananas

1 3/4 cups sifted cake flour
3/4 teaspoon salt
2 teaspoons baking powder
1/4 teaspoon soda

Beat egg slightly; stir in salad oil and sugar. Add mashed bananas and mix well. Sift flour with salt, baking powder and soda; add to banana mixture and stir just until liquid and dry ingredients are combined. Fill greased muffin pans two-thirds full. Bake. Temperature: 375°F. Time: 18-20 minutes. Makes 12 muffins.

Pan-Fried Teriyaki Salmon

Teriyaki sauce can add a wonderful flavor to nearly any meat. That is especially true of this recipe when the sauce is drizzled over moist, pan-fried fish fillet.

This is also the perfect dish to serve a large, hungry crowd—just place the salmon on a baking pan lined with greased foil and bake as many pieces of fish that will fit on the pan all at once.

YIELD: 4 SERVINGS

**4 salmon steaks or fillets
   (4 oz. each)**
Canola oil

TERIYAKI SAUCE:

¼ cup brown sugar, packed
¼ cup soy sauce
⅓ cup mirin (sweet rice wine)
1 teaspoon grated fresh ginger

Combine Teriyaki Sauce ingredients in saucepan; heat until sugar dissolves; set aside.

Pat-dry salmon pieces with damp paper towel. Fry fish in hot oil until browned and opague on both sides. Brush Teriyaki Sauce on salmon; plate then drizzle more just before serving.

Dynamite Seafood Salad

A variation of a popular pūpū found here in the Islands, this recipe reminds me of my parents' brief tenure as proprietors of Hananoya, a Japanese teahouse in Honolulu where Dad's specialty was Baked Lobster Salad served in a lobster shell. With its creamy and delicious mayonnaise dressing, it truly lived up to the local expression, "Broke da mouth!"

Combine all ingredients, except paprika, in medium bowl; toss to combine well.

Sprinkle paprika on top. Place mixture in casserole. Bake, uncovered, at 375°F for 20 to 30 minutes or until heated through. Serve hot or cold.

YIELD: ABOUT 6 SERVINGS

1 cup shellfish (crab, lobster or shrimp), chopped or shredded
½ cup minced onion
¼ cup minced celery
2 cups cabbage, finely shredded
1 cup mayonnaise (more or less to taste)
Salt and pepper to taste
Paprika

Mom & Dad, circa 1960s (Muriel Miura)

Hawaiian Curry

YIELD: 6 TO 8 SERVINGS

1 small onion, minced
1 clove garlic, minced
1 slice fresh ginger root, minced
2 tablespoons canola oil
⅓ cup flour
1 tablespoon curry powder
1 teaspoon salt
2½ cups chicken or beef broth
1 cup coconut milk
½ cup evaporated milk, undiluted
2 cups cooked chicken, shrimps, crab or beef, cubed
2 tablespoons sherry

Ahhhh…memories. I first learned of the preparation of this dish as a home economics student. It was the centerpiece of a formal dinner. In those days meals were much more formal. The table was usually set using fine linens, silverware and china for guests, giving the table a nice look of refinement.

Sauté onion, garlic and ginger in hot oil; cover and cook until onion is translucent. Add flour, curry powder and salt; stir until smooth. Slowly stir in broth and coconut milk; taste and add more curry, if desired. Cover and simmer on low heat, stirring frequently, for about 45 minutes or until thickened. Add cooked meat, chicken or seafood and cook just long enough to heat through. Just before serving, add sherry. Adjust flavor, as desired. Serve over hot steamed rice with any or all of the following condiments:

- Chutney
- Chopped raisins
- Chopped peanuts or macadamia nuts
- Minced green onion
- Shredded coconut
- Chopped sweet pickle
- Crisp crumbled bacon
- Chopped hard cooked eggs

VARIATION:

VEGETARIAN CURRY: Omit chicken, beef and seafood from recipe; substitute vegetable broth for chicken or beef broth. Do not serve bacon as condiment.

Lemongrass Shrimp

*L*emongrass and nuoc mam give this scrumptious dish a decidedly exotic flavor. This dish goes well with hot steamed rice or can serve as a topping for salads.

Heat oil in large skillet; stir-fry shallots and garlic over medium-high heat until fragrant, about 30 seconds. Add the shrimp and lemongrass; stir-fry for about 2 minutes. Add mushrooms, fish sauce, sugar and salt; stir-fry until shrimp is cooked and mushrooms are wilted. Serve hot with rice or warm over Bun (see Lemongrass Bun on page 138).

(see Lemongrass Bun on page 138).

YIELD: 4 SERVINGS

2 tablespoons canola oil
2 shallots, thinly sliced
1 clove garlic, minced
1 pound large shrimp, peeled and deveined
1 tablespoon minced fresh lemongrass
2 cups sliced white mushrooms
2 teaspoons nuoc mam (fish sauce)
1 teaspoon sugar
Salt to taste

NOODLE SALAD:

- 2 cups romaine or green leaf lettuce, washed and shredded
- 2 cups bean sprouts, washed and drained
- 1½ cups cucumber, julienned
- ¼ cup mint leaves, coarsely chopped
- 2 tablespoons small or Thai basil leaves, coarsely chopped
- 1 package (8 oz.) rice vermicelli (rice sticks), cook as directed on package
- 1 recipe Lemongrass Shrimp (see page 137)

GARNISHES:

- 3 tablespoons chopped roasted peanuts
- Cilantro

NUOC CHAM (VIETNAMESE DIPPING SAUCE):
YIELD: ABOUT 1 ½ CUPS

- 1 small jalapeño chile, minced
- 1 clove garlic, minced or pressed
- ½ teaspoon ground chile paste (more or less to taste)
- ⅔ cup hot water
- ¼ cup sugar
- ¼ cup nuoc mam (fish sauce)*
- 2 tablespoons lime juice
- 2 tablespoons shredded carrots, optional

Chile paste and fish sauce are available at Asian grocery stores or in the oriental section of some supermarkets.

Lemongrass Bun
(Vietnamese Noodle Salad)

Bun is a traditional Vietnamese dish made from rice noodles. The noodles sit on a bed of crisp lettuce, bean sprouts, cucumbers, basil and mint, and then are topped with a variety of toppings from spring rolls to lemongrass shrimp. It is an intricately flavored dish of contrasting tastes and textures and sure to be a crowd pleaser.

Arrange lettuce, bean sprouts, cucumbers, mint leaves, basil and cooked vermicelli, which has been well-drained, or divide all ingredients into 6 to 8 individual bowls in a large chilled bowl. Prepare Lemongrass Shrimp or other desired topping and place on top of noodles; garnish with roasted peanuts and cilantro. Each diner can drizzle salad with desired amount of Nuoc Cham which is served on the side.

NUOC CHAM (VIETNAMESE DIPPING SAUCE):

Combine all ingredients in a jar; cover and shake well. Let stand for at least 20 minutes before using. This sauce may be used for most Vietnamese dishes. Keep sauce refrigerated; it can last for a month.

Baked Gon Lo Mein

No party or gathering in Hawai'i would be complete without a noodle dish. This recipe is tasty and easy to prepare!

In 9 x 13 x 2-inch pan mix noodles with vegetables, char siu or ham, and sesame seeds. Toss with oyster sauce and sesame oil. Cover tightly with foil. Bake at 350°F for 15 to 20 minutes or until heated through. Sprinkle with Chinese parsley when ready to serve.

TIP: Cooked thick spaghetti noodles may be substituted for chow mein noodles. Chow mein noodles are available at Asian grocery stores or the Oriental sections of some supermarkets.

YIELD: 4-6 SERVINGS

1 package (12 oz.) chow mein
   noodles
1 package (10 oz.) bean sprouts
1 cup sliced celery
½ cup green onion, cut into
   ½-inch lengths
1 cup slice char siu or ham
1 tablespoon toasted sesame
   seeds
2½ tablespoons oyster sauce
1 tablespoon sesame oil
Chinese parsley for garnish

Chinatown, circa 1980 (Bishop Museum)

Spaghetti with Bolognese Sauce

A terrific blend of broth, tomato paste, vegetables, and cured meats, gives this classic Bolognese Sauce a hearty flavor that accents the pasta nicely. This dish is sure to be a favorite.

Heat oil in medium casserole; add garlic, pancetta, carrot, onion and celery. Cook over moderately low heat, stirring occasionally until onion is golden, about 5 minutes. Add ground beef and pork; cook over moderate heat, breaking up the meat with wooden spoon until no pink remains, about 8 minutes. Stir in tomato paste and cook 2 minutes. Add wine and cook, stirring frequently until reduced by half, about 3 minutes. Add tomatoes and their juices, chicken or beef broth, and 1 tablespoon each of parsley and basil; bring to a boil. Season to taste with salt and pepper; cover and simmer over low heat, stirring occasionally until very thick, about 1½ hours. Keep warm.

Just before serving, stir in the cream and the remaining 2 tablespoons of parsley and 1 tablespoon of basil into the meat sauce. Adjust seasoning to taste; add 2 cups to the spaghetti which should be cooked to al dente and drained. Toss. Transfer the spaghetti to a large pasta bowl, top with the remaining sauce and serve. Pass the Parmesan cheese at the table. Great when served with hot garlic bread.

TIP: The Bolognese sauce can be made and refrigerated for up to 5 days.

YIELD: 6 SERVINGS

2 tablespoons extra-virgin olive oil
3 cloves garlic, minced
3 ounces thinly sliced pancetta, chopped
1 medium carrot, finely diced
1 medium onion, minced
1 rib celery, finely diced
1 pound coarsely ground beef
1 pound coarsely ground pork
1 tablespoon tomato paste
1 cup dry white wine
1 can (28 oz.) whole tomatoes, chopped, juices reserved
1½ cup chicken or beef broth
3 tablespoons chopped flat-leaf parsley
2 tablespoons chopped basil
Salt and freshly ground pepper to taste
1 pound spaghetti
¼ cup heavy cream
Freshly grated Parmesan cheese

Pasta Casserole

An easy and tasty dish perfect for a casual evening at home with friends and family, this casserole can be made well ahead of time and needs only a crisp Island garden salad to complete the meal.

YIELD: 6 SERVINGS

4 cups (8 oz.) uncooked wagon wheel pasta
¾ pound Italian sausage, sliced
1 can (4 oz.) mushroom stems and pieces, drained
1 jar (28 oz.) spaghetti sauce
1 cup (4 oz.) shredded mozzarella cheese

Cook and drain pasta as directed on package. While pasta is cooking, sauté sausage in skillet over medium-high heat, stirring occasionally, until no longer pink; drain. Mix pasta, sausage and remaining ingredients except cheese in ungreased 2½ quart casserole; cover. Bake at 350°F for 30 minutes, or until hot and bubbly. Sprinkle with cheese. Bake, uncovered, additional 5 minutes or until cheese is melted.

VARIATION: Any type of pasta may be substituted for the wagon wheel pasta.

Pansit *(Filipino-Style Fried Noodles)*

Soak rice noodles in cold water for 30 minutes or until softened. Sauté garlic in hot oil until slightly browned; remove and discard. Add pork and sauté over medium heat, stirring frequently, 4 to 5 minutes. Add chicken and sauté 2 to 3 minutes. Add shrimp and sauté another 2 to 3 minutes. Add celery and seasonings; cook 2 to 3 minutes.

Drain rice noodles and cut in 4-inch lengths. Add to meat mixture and continue cooking, stirring frequently, until noodles are heated through, about 2 to 3 minutes. Place on large serving platter. Sprinkle with green onions and arrange alternate wedges of lime and egg around. Serve hot with lime juice and soy sauce.

YIELD: 4-6 SERVINGS

½ pound rice noodles (bijon or rice sticks)
3 tablespoons canola oil
2 cloves garlic, crushed
¾ pound pork, cut in thin strips
½ boneless chicken, cut in thin strips
¼ pound shrimp, cleaned and diced
½ cup sliced celery
2 teaspoons salt
Fresh ground pepper to taste

GARNISH:

½ cup chopped green onion
3 limes, quartered
3 hard-boiled eggs, quartered

For more recipes and ideas, see Muriel Miura's book, Hawai'i's Party Food.

WOW...a Treasury of Desserts

A good dessert is the ultimate goal of any meal. It is the sweet ending everyone at the table is working towards. A meal seems somewhat diminished without dessert.

Here is a treasury of desserts to add to your collection. Some of them have been pleasing people for decades, and some are new. They are all relatively easy to prepare and each one tastes scrumptious and satisfying!

Muriel with daughter on first birthday, 1961
(Muriel Miura)

Just Chocolate...

No matter what your chocolate preference—smooth, rich milk chocolate or the slightly bitter, but no less decadent, dark chocolate—one of the following recipes is sure to suit your craving.

Chocolate, the most popular dessert flavor, was introduced to the American colonies in 1693 as a rich and creamy beverage. This worldly delight swept the country and Americans fell in love with this velvety, smooth sensation. The desire to consume chocolate in other forms was overwhelming. Chefs everywhere began experimenting with this enticing ingredient.

In 1911, the first candy bar—a perfect combination of the decadent chocolate taste and ready-to-eat convenience—was introduced to America. In the 1930s, a clever woman broke a solid chocolate bar into pieces and added them to her ordinary cookie dough. And the chocolate chip cookie was born. Through the years, chocolate has become more than just a simple beverage, a melt-in-your mouth candy bar, or warm and gooey chips in cookies. Chocolate became a classic loved by many.

Create your own delectable chocolate treasures of breads, cakes, candies, and cookies—the possibilities are endless. To help you achieve chocolate perfection, here are some tips:

MELTING CHOCOLATE

- **Stove top**: Place chopped chocolate in a dry heat-proof bowl over simmering water; stir chocolate until smooth. Don't let any water in the bowl or the chocolate will "seize" and become grainy. If this happens, add ½ teaspoon shortening (not butter) for each ounce of chocolate and stir until smooth. Chocolate scorches easily, and once scorched cannot be used.
- **Microwave**: Place chopped chocolate in microwave-safe container. Microwave on medium/low setting in one-minute bursts, stirring after each session. When the chocolate seems two-thirds melted, stir to melt the remaining chocolate since it will continue to cook after the bowl is removed from microwave oven.

STORING

Chocolate will keep for a year at room temperature. It's best to keep it wrapped in foil or waxed paper and stored below 70ºF away from strong smelling foods. Bittersweet and semisweet chocolate can be stored for years whereas milk chocolate should be used within nine months because they contain milk solids.

GENERAL GUIDELINES

- Read the entire recipe before beginning to make sure you have all the necessary ingredients and utensils.
- Remove butter, margarine and cream cheese from the refrigerator to soften, if necessary.
- Toast, chop and grind nuts, peel and slice fruit and melt chocolate before preparing the recipe.

Chocolate Dipped Fruits

hocolate-covered fruits taste wonderful and make a lovely presentation. Be sure, however, to eat these delectable treats within 24 hours following preparation to avoid spoilage.

Semisweet or sweet bar chocolate, cut up and melt over very low heat or microwave.

Wash fruits, leaving stems and leaves on whole fruits. Dry fruit surfaces as much as possible. Using toothpicks to hold fruits, dip fruits into the melted chocolate, then wipe off excess against edge of pan. If possible, place the other end of the toothpicks in a piece of styrofoam to allow fruits to dry upside down.

YIELD: VARIES

SUGGESTED FRUITS:

Strawberries
Raspberries
Cherries
Grapes
Tangerine Sections
Orange Sections
Bananas
Apple Slices
Pear Slices

Chocolate Cream Cheese Éclairs

TO MAKE ECLAIRS: In saucepan, melt butter in boiling water. Add flour and salt and stir vigorously. Cook over low heat, stirring constantly, until mixture forms a ball in the pan.

Cool slightly. Add eggs, one at a time, beating well after each addition, until smooth.

Using pastry bag, form ¾ x 3-inch strips of dough 3 inches apart on lightly greased baking pan. Bake at 400°F for 45 to 50 minutes or until well-browned. Remove éclairs from oven; split and remove any filaments of soft dough. Turn oven off and return éclairs to oven to dry out, about 20 minutes. Cool completely. Fill centers with Chocolate Cream Cheese Filling just before serving. Drizzle Chocolate Glaze on each éclair to serve.

TO MAKE CHOCOLATE CREAM CHEESE FILLING: Heat chocolate chips in small saucepan over low heat, stirring occasionally, until melted; cool. Beat cream cheese, sugar, milk and vanilla extract until smooth. Stir in melted chocolate. Beat heavy cream until soft peaks form; fold into chocolate mixture. Fill éclair (or cream puff) shells.

TO MAKE CHOCOLATE GLAZE: Combine confectioner's sugar and cocoa; mix well. Stir in milk and mix until smooth. If necessary, add more milk, ½ teaspoon at a time, until of desired consistency.

VARIATIONS:

CREAM PUFFS: The Éclair puff pastry (Pate A Chou) can also be used to make cream puffs. Drop rounded tablespoons of dough, 3 inches apart, on lightly greased baking pan. Follow directions for Éclairs.

CREAM CUSTARD FILLING: Combine ½ cup sugar, ¼ teaspoon salt, and 2½ tablespoons cornstarch in saucepan. Add 2 beaten eggs, stirring until well-blended. Slowly stir in 2 cups scalded milk, and cook mixture over low heat, stirring constantly, until mixture thickens. Add butter and vanilla extract. Cool before filling Cream Puffs or Éclairs. Drizzle with Chocolate Glaze to serve.

PATE A CHOU/ÉCLAIRS:

YIELD: 8-10 ÉCLAIRS

½ cup butter or margarine
1 cup boiling water
1 cup flour
½ teaspoon salt
4 eggs
Chocolate Cream Cheese Filling (recipe below)
Chocolate Glaze (recipe below)

CHOCOLATE CREAM CHEESE FILLING:

YIELD: ABOUT 2 CUPS

¼ cup semisweet chocolate chips
1 package (3 oz.) cream cheese, softened
⅓ cup brown sugar, packed
¼ cup milk
½ teaspoon vanilla extract
1 cup chilled heavy cream

CHOCOLATE GLAZE:

YIELD: ABOUT ¾ CUP

1 cup confectioner's sugar
2 tablespoons cocoa
2 tablespoons milk

Lava Cake

A chocolate cake by itself is a treat, but a chocolate cake with a soft chocolate center is decadence personified! What's more, this dessert is simple and easy to prepare. The batter can be prepared the day before, refrigerated and baked just before serving.

YIELD: 6 SERVINGS

1 package (6 squares) bittersweet baking chocolate (Valrohna, Scharffen Berger preferred), break into pieces
¼ pound (½ cup) butter, cut into chunks
1½ cups confectioner's sugar
½ cup flour
3 whole eggs
3 egg yolks

SUGGESTED GARNISHES:

Sweetened whipped cream
Ice cream
6 fresh raspberries

Grease six 6-ounce ovenproof custard cups, ramekins or soufflé dishes. Place on baking sheet; set aside.

Microwave chocolate and butter in large microwaveable bowl on HIGH 1 minute or MEDIUM (50%) 2 minutes or until butter is melted. Stir with wire whisk until chocolate is completely melted. Add sugar and flour; mix well. Whisk in whole eggs and egg yolks; beat until well blended. Divide batter evenly into prepared ovenproof dishes. Bake at 425°F for 10 to 14 minutes, or until cakes are firm around the edges but still soft in the centers. Let stand 1 minute. Run small knife around cakes to loosen. Invert cakes carefully onto dessert dishes. To serve, cut in half, if desired; garnish with additional powdered sugar lightly sprinkled, dollop of sweetened whipped cream or ice cream and top with fresh raspberries. Serve warm.

FLAVOR VARIATIONS: Prepare as directed. Add 1 teaspoon pure almond extract, orange extract, vanilla extract, raspberry extract or ground cinnamon to batter. If desired, prepare batter day before and pour into prepared cups or dishes; cover with plastic wrap; refrigerate. Bring to room temperature when ready to serve, uncover and bake as directed.

Tunnel of Fudge Cake

An updated version on a prize-winning dessert from 1966, this walnut-studded pound cake has the consistency of a brownie with a gooey, fudge center. It's a classic that can't be beat.

YIELD: ABOUT 16 SERVINGS

1¾ cups (3½ sticks) butter
or margarine, at room
temperature
6 eggs
1¾ cups granulated sugar
2 cups confectioner's sugar
2¼ cups flour
¾ cup cocoa (American style,
not Dutch process)
2 cups coarsely chopped
walnuts

GLAZE (OPTIONAL):

¾ cup confectioner's sugar
¼ cup cocoa
1½ to 2 tablespoons milk

Grease and flour a 12-cup fluted tube (bundt) pan or 10-inch angel food tube pan. Set aside.

In a large bowl, beat the butter or margarine and granulated sugar until light and fluffy. Add eggs one at a time, beating well after each addition. Gradually add the confectioner's sugar, blending well. Using a wooden spoon, stir in the confectioner's sugar, flour, cocoa and walnuts until well blended. Spoon the batter in the prepared pan; spread evenly. Bake at 350°F for 58 to 62 minutes*. Cool upright in pan for 1 hour. Remove cake from pan and cool on a rack for another hour. Turn cake out onto a serving platter and let cool completely. If desired, glaze cake when fully cooled. To make glaze, combine the Glaze ingredients in a small bowl and mix until well-blended. Spoon over top of cake, allowing some to run down sides. Store cake tightly covered. Best served warm.

TIP: * Since the cake has a soft tunnel of fudge, ordinary doneness tests can't be used. Accurate oven temperature and baking time are crucial. The lesser time will result in a more wet center, which is fine. The longer baking time may result in a too-dry texture.

Chocolate Mayonnaise Cake

*M*ayonnaise in a cake might seem a bit odd, but it lends a richness and moistness to the recipe. This dish first became popular in the 1960s when it first appeared on the labels of mayonnaise jars across the country and it has been a much sought after recipe ever since.

Grease and flour bottoms of two 9-inch round cake pans; set aside.

In a medium-sized bowl, stir together flour, cocoa, baking soda and baking powder; set aside. In large bowl beat sugar, eggs and vanilla extract at high speed using mixer, occasionally scraping bowl, 3 minutes or until light and fluffy. Reduce speed to low, beat in mayonnaise. Add flour mixture in 4 additions alternately with water, beginning and ending with flour. Pour batter into prepared pans. Bake at 350°F for 30 to 35 minutes, or until cake tester inserted in center comes out clean. Cool in pans 10 minutes; remove and cool on wire racks. Frost as desired.

YIELD: TWO 9-INCH LAYERS

2 cups flour
⅓ cup unsweetened cocoa
1¼ teaspoons baking soda
¼ teaspoon baking powder
1⅔ cups sugar
3 eggs
1 teaspoon vanilla extract
1 cup real mayonnaise
1⅓ cup water

Chocolate Fudge Sauce

*C*hocolate Fudge Sauce is a perfect addition to any dessert. This sauce is easy to prepare and enhances the flavor of whatever sweets you decide to drizzle it over.

Melt chocolate and butter slowly in heavy saucepan over low heat. Meanwhile, heat water to boiling. When chocolate mixture has melted, add water and stir until well blended. Add sugar and corn syrup; mix until smooth. Turn heat up to medium and while stirring constantly, bring mixture to a boil; adjust heat so that sauce is maintained at the boiling point. Allow sauce to boil, without stirring, for 9 minutes. Remove sauce from heat and cool 15 minutes. Stir in rum, if desired. Serve warm over ice cream, profiteroles or cake slices.

YIELD: 2½ CUPS

4 ounces unsweetened chocolate
3 tablespoons butter
⅔ cup water
1½ cups sugar
6 tablespoons corn syrup
1 tablespoon rum, optional

German Chocolate Cake

he history of the German Chocolate Cake is a bit muddled. The recipe is not actually German at all, but first appeared in a Dallas newspaper in the 1950s. Food historians speculate that the cake took its name from the particular brand of chocolate bar used in the dish produced by an Englishman named Sam German. Whatever the origin, this cake has become a delicious mainstay on dining tables across the United States.

YIELD: 3-LAYER 9-INCH CAKE

1 package (4 oz.) German sweet chocolate
½ cup boiling water
2½ cups sifted cake flour
1 teaspoon baking soda
½ teaspoon salt
1 cup butter or margarine
2 cups sugar
4 egg yolks
1 teaspoon vanilla extract
1 cup buttermilk
4 egg whites
Coconut-Pecan Filling and Frosting (see page 155)

Melt chocolate in boiling water; cool. Sift flour with soda and salt. Cream butter and sugar until light and fluffy. Add egg yolks one at a time, beating well after each addition. Blend in vanilla extract and melted chocolate. Add flour mixture alternately with the buttermilk, beating well after each addition, until smooth. Beat egg whites until soft peaks form; fold into batter. Pour batter into three 9-inch layer pans which have been lined on bottoms with paper. Bake at 350°F for 30 to 35 minutes, or until cake springs back when lightly pressed in center. Cool cake in pans 15 minutes; remove from pan and finish cooling on rack. Spread Coconut-Pecan Filling and Frosting between layers and top of cake.

NOTE: This delicate cake will have a flat slightly sugary top crust which tends to crack.

Coconut-Pecan Filling and Frosting

This rich, butterscotch-flavored frosting is a perfect complement to any chocolate or yellow cake. Pecans and coconut make terrific accents for this recipe, but may be left out of the final dish if so desired.

Combine milk, sugar, egg yolks, butter and vanilla extract in a saucepan. Cook over medium heat, stirring occasionally until mixture thickens, about 10 to 12 minutes. Remove from heat. Add coconut and pecans. Cool to desired consistency, beating occasionally. Makes enough to cover tops of three 9-inch layers.

TIP: For thinner frosting, use only 2 egg yolks.

YIELD: ABOUT 2 ½ CUPS

1 cup evaporated milk or
    heavy cream
1 cup sugar
3 egg yolks, slightly beaten
½ cup butter or margarine
1 teaspoon vanilla extract
1⅓ cups shredded coconut
1 cup chopped pecans

Chocolate Bread Pudding

Bread pudding is a perfect and delicious way to dispense with any leftover bread you might have left in your kitchen. Virtually any bread or roll will do. Do not, however, use muffins or biscuits as these are not leavened with yeast and do not work well with this recipe.

YIELD: 10 TO 12 SERVINGS

- 1 pound (6-7 cups) stale Portuguese sweet bread, brioche, or challah bread cubes
- 1 cup heavy cream
- ¾ cup sugar
- ¼ teaspoon salt
- 1 package (12 oz.) bittersweet or semisweet chocolate morsels, chopped
- 4 large eggs
- 2 cups milk
- 1 tablespoon vanilla extract
- ¼ cup butter or margarine, softened

Cut bread into ½-inch thick slices then into ½-inch cubes, making 6 to 7 cups; set aside. Combine cream, sugar and salt in saucepan; bring to a boil, stirring constantly. Remove from heat then add chocolate pieces. Let stand 2 minutes, then whisk until smooth. In large bowl, whisk together eggs; add milk and vanilla extract. Whisk in the chocolate mixture, then stir in bread cubes thoroughly to moisten. Let stand 1 to 2 hours, gently stirring and pressing bread down occasionally with spatula to help absorb the liquid.

Pour mixture into generously buttered 2-quart baking dish or pan; smooth top of pudding and dot with butter or margarine. Bake at 325°F for 50 to 60 minutes, or until knife inserted in center comes out clean. Let cool for 45 minutes, then cut and serve with drizzle of chocolate sauce of choice or scoop of ice cream.

VARIATIONS:
- Add chopped dried fruits, toasted nuts, chocolate chips, orange or lemon zest
- Add few tablespoon of bourbon, brandy or rum.
- Omit chopped chocolate.
- Use maple or lemon extracts
- Serve with maple syrup, vanilla extract custard, or melted jams.
- Serve with scoop of ice cream; drizzle with sauce of choice.

TIP: Bread puddings can be covered and refrigerated for up to 3 days.

Cakes & Frostings

A festive occasion—be it a wedding, birthday, anniversary, or holiday—calls for a festive cake. The following easy-to-follow recipes will help you to prepare a delicious homemade cake sure to please any crowd.

Macadamia Nut Chiffon Cake

Chiffon cakes are as light as angel food cakse yet have the richness of a butter cakes. They're popular among homemakers because they're relatively easy to make.

Beat egg whites until foamy; gradually beat in ½ cup sugar until stiff and glossy.

Sift together flour, cinnamon and salt. Combine egg yolks, vanilla extract and remaining sugar; beat until thick and lemon-colored. Stir in dry ingredients. Pour batter into egg whites and fold in gently, but thoroughly. Fold in nuts.

Pour into ungreased 10-inch tube pan. Bake at 350°F for 50-60 minutes. Invert to cool; cool completely before removing from pan. Sprinkle with confectioner's sugar or top with sweetened whipped cream to serve.

VARIATION: Substitute walnuts for macadamia nuts.

YIELD: 8-10 SERVINGS

9 egg whites (1¼ cups)
1½ cups sugar
¾ cup flour
1½ teaspoons ground
   cinnamon
1 teaspoon salt
9 egg yolks
1½ teaspoons vanilla extract
2 cups macadamia nuts, very
   finely chopped or ground

Coconut Cake

A *slightly different take on the classic coconut cake, this recipe uses coconut not only in the frosting, but also in the batter. This gives the cake a wonderful flaky texture. It's delicious, too. Give it a try!*

Measure sifted flour, baking powder and salt; sift together. Cream together butter and sugar until light and fluffy. Add eggs one at a time, beating well after each addition. Add flour mixture and milk in alternating additions, beating well after each addition until smooth. Stir in vanilla extract and coconut. Pour batter into two 8-inch greased and floured layer pans. Bake at 350°F for 30 to 35 minutes or until done. Cool in pans 10 minutes; then remove from pans and finish cooling on racks. Frost with Haupia Frosting (see below) or sweetened whipped cream to serve.

YIELD: TWO LAYER 8-INCH CAKE

1¾ cups sifted cake flour
2¼ teaspoons baking powder
¾ teaspoon salt
½ cup butter or margarine
1 cup plus 2 tablespoons sugar
2 eggs
⅔ cup milk
1 teaspoon vanilla extract
⅔ cup Angel Flake coconut

Haupia Frosting

H *aupia is the coconut pudding often served as dessert at a lūʻau. It also makes a delicious frosting or topping for cakes and other desserts.*

Mix cornstarch with sugar and water in saucepan. Stir in coconut milk and cook over low heat, stirring constantly until mixture thickens. Remove from heat; cool slightly. Spread between layers and on top of cake. Let cool until haupia is firm.

Whip cream until soft peaks form; add sugar slowly and continue beating until stiff peaks form. Spread sweetened whipped cream on top and sides of cake; sprinkle with coconut before serving.

YIELD: ABOUT 2 CUPS

6 tablespoons cornstarch
6 tablespoons sugar
¾ cup water
1 can (12 oz.) frozen coconut milk, thawed
1 cup heavy cream
3 tablespoons sugar
1 package (4 oz.) frozen shredded coconut, thawed

Old Fashioned Prune Cake

One of the fondest memories I have of my mother's kitchen is a little stack of index cards with recipes hand-written, bound together with a rubber band, neatly stacked in the corner of a drawer. Mom was not really a baker but she especially treasured this Prune Cake recipe given to her by her sister. The "groom's cake" or favors at weddings in the "old days" used to be a piece of prune cake neatly wrapped with a beautiful bow rather than the elaborate favors of today.

YIELD: 8-10 SERVINGS

1 cup sugar
1 cup butter, softened
2 eggs
1 teaspoon vanilla extract
1 cup prune pulp
1½ cups cake flour
1½ teaspoons baking soda
1 teaspoon ground cinnamon
½ teaspoon ground cloves
½ teaspoon salt
½ cup buttermilk or sour milk
½ cup macadamia nuts, chopped

Cream sugar and butter until light and fluffy. Add eggs one at a time, beating well after each addition. Add vanilla extract. Beat in prune pulp.

Sift together flour, baking soda, cinnamon, cloves and salt. Add dry ingredients and buttermilk in alternate, beginning and ending with dry ingredients. Stir in nuts.

Pour into 2 greased 9-inch layer pans or a 9-inch tube pan. Bake at 350°F for 30 to 35 minutes for 9-inch layers, or 1 hour for tube pan or until cake tests done. Frost with Prune Frosting (recipe follows) or sprinkle with sifted confectioner's sugar, if desired.

TIPS:
- Add ½ teaspoon vinegar to ½ cup milk to make sour milk.
- Cover dried, pitted prunes with water in saucepan; simmer until tender; mash or pulverize in blender. Today's prunes are vacuum packed and tender so stewing may not be necessary.

Prune Frosting

YIELD: ABOUT 1 ½ CUPS

½ cup butter, softened
3 cups confectioner's sugar, sifted
3 tablespoons milk
½ cup minced, stewed prunes
½ teaspoon lemon extract

Cream butter and sugar until light and fluffy. Add milk, prunes and lemon extract; continue beating until mixture is well blended and fluffy. Frost cake.

Liliko'i Pudding Cakes

The dry ingredients are overwhelmed with the wet ones. When the cake finishes baking, an amazing texture separation takes place and you'll have a dessert with a layer of light cake and a layer of rich passion fruit pudding. 'Ono!

Spray six 6-oz. ramekins with vegetable oil spray. In a medium bowl, whisk sugar with flour. In another bowl whisk egg yolks with butter until well blended. Whisk in the milk, liliko'i juice and lemon zest. Pour the liliko'i mixture into the sugar mixture and whisk until smooth.

In medium bowl, beat egg whites with the salt until firm peaks form. Gently fold the egg whites into the liliko'i mixture. Pour batter into prepared ramekins and transfer them to a small roasting pan. Place the pan in the oven and pour in enough water to reach halfway up the sides of the ramekins. Bake at 350°F for 35 minutes, or until puffy and golden brown on top. Serve cakes in ramekins. Or run knife around edge of each cake and invert onto dessert plates. Serve warm or at room temperature with the diced fruits.

TIP: If fresh liliko'i juice concentrate is used, increase sugar to ¾ cup.

YIELD: 6 CAKES

½ cup sugar
⅓ cup flour
3 large eggs, separated
2 tablespoons unsalted butter, softened
1 cup milk
⅓ cup frozen liliko'i juice concentrate, thawed
1 teaspoon grated lemon zest
¼ teaspoon salt
Diced fresh fruit for garnish

Tomato Spice Cake

Tomato sauce might not seem like an ingredient that belongs in a cake, but the results are moist, delicate and delicious.

YIELD: 12-16 SERVINGS

3 cups flour, sifted
1 tablespoon baking powder
1 teaspoon cinnamon
½ teaspoon nutmeg
¼ teaspoon cloves
¾ cup shortening
1 ¼ cups sugar
2 eggs
1 can (10¾ oz.) condensed tomato sauce
¾ cup water
1 teaspoon baking soda
1 cup chopped nuts (macadamia, pecan, walnuts)
½ cup raisins, optional

Sift flour, baking powder, cinnamon, nutmeg, cloves. Cream shortening and sugar together until light and fluffy. Add eggs one at a time, beating well after each addition. Combine tomato soup, water and baking soda. Add dry ingredients and soup mixture alternately to creamed mixture, starting and ending with dry ingredients. Stir in nuts and raisins.

Pour batter into a greased and floured or waxed paper-lined 9x13-inch, or sheet pan 8 or 9-inch layer pans. Bake at 350°F for 30 to 35 minutes or until done. Cool and frost with Cream Cheese Frosting (see page 164).

VARIATIONS:

BUNDT CAKE: Bake in well-greased and lightly floured 2½ quart Bundt pan for 50 to 60 minutes. Cool right-side-up in pan for 15 minutes; remove from pan. Cool. If desired, sprinkle with confectioner's sugar instead of frosting.

EASY TOMATO SPICE CAKE: Blend in large bowl 1 box (18.25 oz.) spice cake mix, 1 can (10¾ oz.) condensed tomato soup combined with enough water to make 1⅓ cups liquid, 2 eggs and 1/3 cup canola oil at low speed until moistened (about 30 seconds). Beat at medium speed for 1 to 2 minutes; pour into prepared pans and bake according to directions above.

Cream Cheese Frosting

YIELD: ABOUT 3 CUPS

1 package (8 oz.) cream cheese,
   softened
2 tablespoons evaporated milk
1 teaspoon vanilla extract
1 box (16 oz.) confectioner's
   sugar, sifted

Combine cream cheese, milk and vanilla extract in medium bowl; beat until light and fluffy. Slowly beat in confectioner's sugar until smooth and to spreadable consistency. Add more milk if necessary, ½ teaspoon at a time, until desired consistency. Frost cake.

Yellow Chiffon Cake

One of my favorites, I use this recipe whenever I need to bake a cake . It pairs so well with any type of frosting or topping.

**YIELD: TWO-LAYER
8-INCH CAKE**

2 eggs, separated
1½ cups sugar
2¼ cups sifted cake flour
1 tablespoon baking powder
1 teaspoon salt
⅓ cup salad oil
1 cup milk
1½ teaspoons vanilla extract

Beat egg whites until frothy. Gradually beat in ½ cup sugar; continue beating until very stiff and glossy.

Sift together remaining sugar, flour, baking powder and salt. Add salad oil, half of milk and vanilla. Beat 1 minute, medium speed on mixer or 150 strokes. Add remaining milk and egg yolks; beat 1 minute more. Fold in meringue. Pour into two greased and floured 8-inch layer cake pans. Bake at 350°F for 30 to 35 minutes. Cool. Frost with favorite frosting to serve.

Butter Pound Cake

Old pound cake recipes literally called for a pound of butter, sugar, and flour...In these health conscious times, bakers have had to scale back. Still, this modified pound cake recipe sacrifices none of the rich flavor. Pound cakes also keep well and can be stored and frozen. It's always good to have one on hand in the freezer in case an unexpected guest pops by.

Cream butter and sugar together until light and fluffy. Add vanilla extract. Add eggs one at a time, beating well after each addition. Sift together dry ingredients. Add to creamed mixture alternately with milk, beginning and ending with dry mixture. Pour into sprayed or greased and floured 10-inch tube pan. Bake at 350°F for 1 hour, or until toothpick inserted comes out clean. Cool in pan 5 minutes; turn out onto wire rack to cool. Sift confectioner's sugar over top.

VARIATIONS:

LEMON POUND CAKE: Substitute 1 teaspoon lemon extract for the vanilla extract. Fold 3 teaspoons lemon zest into batter.

MACADAMIA NUT POUND CAKE: Omit vanilla extract. Add 2 teaspoons ground cinnamon with the flour. Fold in 1¼ cups toasted macadamia nut bits into batter.

ORANGE COCONUT POUND CAKE: Fold 1⅓ cups flaked coconut and 2 to 3 tablespoons orange zest into batter.

SERVING SUGGESTIONS:
- Butter cake slices; broil until light brown; top with ice cream, drizzle with caramel topping and top with chopped macadamia nuts.
- Top cake slices with sweetened whipped cream and fresh berries (strawberry, blueberry, raspberry). Garnish with almond slices or bits of macadamia nuts.

YIELD: 10-12 SERVINGS

1 cup butter
2 cups sugar
1½ teaspoons vanilla extract
4 eggs
3 cups sifted cake flour
1 teaspoon baking powder
1½ teaspoons salt
¾ cup milk
Confectioners' sugar

The Best Pies Ever...

Pies were first brought to this country by English settlers who baked them (known as "pyes" in the old spelling) in long, deep dishes called "coffins." During rough periods, frugal bakers rounded the corners of the "coffin" and made it shallow so that the pie would stretch further. At one time, pies were eaten for breakfast, lunch and dinner.

Lemon Meringue Pie

Created at the turn of the 20th century, lemon pie remains second only to chocolate cake as our all-time favorite dessert. I have a special place in my heart for lemon meringue pie; when I was in elementary school this was the special dessert that my folks used to buy as a treat for the family.

Stir together 1 cup sugar and cornstarch in a 3-quart saucepan. Gradually stir in water until smooth. Stir in egg yolks. Stirring constantly, bring to boil over medium heat and cook 1 minute. Remove from heat. Stir in lemon zest, lemon juice and butter or margarine. Cool. Pour into pastry shell. Beat egg whites until foamy in small bowl wit mixer at high speed. Add ⅓ cup sugar, 1 tablespoon at a time, beating well after each addition. Continue beating until stiff peaks form. Spread some meringue around edge of filling, first touching crust all around, then fill center. Bake at 350°F for 15 minutes or until lightly browned. Cool at room temperature away from draft.

YIELD: 8 SLICES

- 1 cup sugar
- 3 tablespoons corn starch
- 1½ cups cold water
- 3 egg yolks, slightly beaten
- Zest of 1 lemon
- ¼ cup lemon juice
- 1 tablespoon butter or margarine
- 1, 9-inch baked pastry shell
- 3 egg whites
- ⅓ cup sugar

Guava Chiffon Pie

The common guava found in Hawai'i has a unique flowery-fruity flavor and makes a perfect ingredient for desserts. Fresh fruits are rarely available for picking from the roadsides today, but the fruit juice is widely available in markets in cans—either chilled, room temperature, or frozen.

YIELD: 8 SERVINGS

1 envelope unflavored gelatin
¼ cup cold water
4 eggs, separated
¼ cup lemon juice
3 tablespoons sugar
1 teaspoon lemon zest
1 can (6 oz.) frozen guava juice, thawed
Few drops red food coloring
¼ teaspoon salt
⅓ cup sugar
9-inch baked pie shell
Sweetened whipped cream

Soften gelatin in water. Beat egg yolks well. Combine in saucepan egg yolks, lemon juice and the 3 tablespoons sugar. Cook over low heat, stirring constantly, until mixture thickens. Stir in softened gelatin until gelatin is dissolved. Cool slightly; stir in lemon zest, guava juice and food coloring. Refrigerate and chill until mixture begins to congeal slightly. In small bowl, beat egg whites with salt until soft peaks form; gradually beat in the remaining ⅓ cup sugar. Fold in stiffly beaten egg whites into guava mixture. Pour into baked pie shell; chill until firm. Serve with sweetened whipped cream.

Custard Pie ala Hawaiʻi

*D*ue to shortages of fresh milk during the Second World War, Hawaiʻi bakers began to substitute evaporated milk in their recipes. The taste caught on in Island homes. If you're looking to give your custard desserts a distinctive local flavor, I recommend the use of evaporated milk.

Beat eggs slightly; stir in sugar, salt, nutmeg, milk and vanilla extract. Whisk to blend ingredients well. Pour into pie shell. Bake at 425°F for 30 to 40 minutes, or until knife inserted in center of pie comes out clean.

YIELD: 8 SERVINGS

5 eggs, slightly beaten
¾ cup sugar
½ teaspoon salt
¼ teaspoon ground nutmeg
3 cups undiluted evaporated milk
1 teaspoon vanilla extract
9-inch unbaked pie shell

(Ian Gillespie)

Banana Streusel Pie

*T*he banana is a versatile fruit. It's a great source of potassium and other nutrients. It makes a great snack and can be used in various recipes. Here it makes a perfect pie filling.

In a large bowl, combine bananas and lemon juice; let stand 15 to 20 minutes. In a small bowl, combine flour and brown sugar; cut in butter; stir in nuts; set aside.

Add sugar, cinnamon and nutmeg to bananas; toss gently to mix. Put into pie shell. Sprinkle flour mixture evenly over bananas. Bake at 400°F for 40 minutes or until golden brown.

YIELD: 8 SERVINGS

6 cups firm-ripe banana chunks
1½ tablespoons lemon juice
1 cup flour
½ cup brown sugar, packed
½ cup butter or margarine, softened
¼ cup macadamia nut bits
⅓ cup sugar
½ teaspoon ground cinnamon
¼ teaspoon ground nutmeg
9-inch baked pie shell

Grasshopper Pie

YIELD: 8-10 SERVINGS

CRUST:

1 ½ cups chocolate wafer
   crumbs
3 tablespoons melted butter

FILLING:

1 envelope unflavored gelatin
¼ cup cold water
2 cups heavy cream, whipped
3 tablespoons sugar
3 tablespoons crème de
   menthe
3 tablespoons crème de cacao
Few drops green food coloring

This dessert reminds me of my time in college when crème de menthe drinks and desserts were very popular. The flavor is wonderful and refreshing and the presentation with its chocolate crust and mint green filling is most impressive.

Prepare crust by combining chocolate wafer crumbs and butter; press firmly into 9-inch pie pan. Chill.

To prepare filling, sprinkle gelatin over cold water to soften; heat over low heat to dissolve. Whip cream with sugar until stiff peaks form; fold in gelatin and remaining ingredients. Pour into chilled crust; refrigerate until set, about 2 to 3 hours. Serve with additional sweetened whipped cream.

Lemon Chiffon Pie

YIELD: 8-10 SERVINGS

1 envelope unflavored gelatin
1 cup sugar, divided
½ teaspoon salt
4 eggs, separated
½ cup fresh lemon juice
⅔ cup water
2 teaspoons lemon zest
1 cup heavy cream, whipped
9-inch baked pie shell
Sweetened whipped cream
Lemon twists, optional

There is nothing like a refreshing lemon pie following a hearty dinner. Try substituting fresh lime for an equally tasty dessert.

Combine gelatin, ½ cup sugar and salt in saucepan. Beat egg yolks with lemon juice and water; stir into gelatin mixture and cook over medium heat, stirring constantly, just until mixture comes to a boil. Cool and refrigerate until partially set.

Beat egg whites until frothy and soft peaks form. Gradually beat in remaining sugar and continue beating until stiff peaks form. Fold into partially set gelatin mixture with lemon zest. Fold in whipped cream and fill pastry shell. Top with additional sweetened whipped cream and lemon twists (if desired) to serve.

Stacked Apple "Pies"

 sweet and simple dessert, this piled-high apple dessert, served with vanilla extract ice cream and caramel sauce, is a novel way to serve your favorite apple pie.

Line a baking sheet with parchment paper. Unroll 1 pie crust onto prepared baking sheet; brush with melted butter and sprinkle with sugar. Using pastry wheel, cut dough into 12 wedges. Bake at 400°F for 12 to 15 minutes or until golden and crisp. Remove from oven; set aside to cool.

Melt remaining butter in nonstick skillet over medium heat; add apples, raisins, cinnamon and salt. Saute about 4 minutes or until apples begin to soften. Add juice; simmer until nearly evaporated; add ¾ cup caramel sauce. Reduce heat to low and keep apple mixture warm.

To assemble, arrange 1 crust wedge on each plate of 6 plates; top each with scoop of ice cream and top with spoonful of apples and caramel sauce. Place second wedge on top with more ice cream and apple mixture. May drizzle additional caramel sauce over apple mixture, if desired. Serve immediately.

TIP: Pastry will shrink during baking and won't stick together so don't bother separating pastry dough after cutting into triangles.

YIELD: ABOUT 6 SERVINGS

1 box refrigerated pie crust*
1 tablespoon butter, melted
2 tablespoons sugar
1 tablespoon unsalted butter
2 Braebum or Pippin apples, peeled, cored, thinly sliced
½ cup golden raisins
¼ teaspoon cinnamon
Pinch of salt
½ cup apple juice
Jar of caramel sauce
Vanilla extract ice cream

* 1 box contains 2 pie crusts. Use 1 crust for this recipe and freeze the remaining dough.

Cookie Fresh Fruit Tarts

Unlike pies that call for two crusts or strudels that hide pie fillings beneath layers of dough, tarts let their colorful and delicious fillings show. These terrific tarts appeal to both the eye and the appetite.

YIELD: VARIES

SUGAR COOKIE CRUST:
YIELD: ABOUT 2½ DOZEN COOKIES

2 cups sugar
1 cup shortening
¾ cup butter or margarine, softened
2 teaspoons vanilla extract
1 egg
3½ cups flour
1 teaspoon baking powder
¼ teaspoon salt
Cream Cheese Spread (see below)
Toppings (sliced fresh fruits, miniature chocolate chips, macadamia nut bits, or jam)

CREAM CHEESE SPREAD:

1 package (8 oz.) cream cheese, softened
½ cup sugar
¾ teaspoon vanilla extract or lemon extract

SUGGESTED FRESH FRUIT TOPPINGS:

Raspberries, Strawberries, Blueberries, Plums, Peaches, Nectarines, Kiwis, Star Fruits

SUGAR COOKIE CRUST: In large mixer bowl, beat sugar with shortening and butter or margarine until light and fluffy; beat in vanilla and egg until well blended. In another bowl, stir together flour, baking powder, and salt; gradually add to butter mixture, blending well, to form a soft dough. Cover with plastic wrap and refrigerate until firm, about 1 to 2 hours or up to 3 days. Roll dough out on floured board, a portion at a time, to ¼-inch thickness (keep remaining portions refrigerated). Cut into rounds with cookie cutter and place slightly apart on ungreased baking sheets. Bake at 400°F for 8 to 10 minutes or until edges are lightly browned. Cool. Store in airtight container until ready for use.

CREAM CHEESE SPREAD: Combine cream cheese, sugar, and lemon or vanilla extract. Beat until soft and well mixed. Spread about 2 teaspoons on each cooled cookie round; top as desired. Place on serving platter and cover with plastic wrap. Keep refrigerated until ready to serve. Eat within 24 hours of preparation.

FRESH FRUIT TOPPINGS: Wash, drain and dry fruits; slice thinly. Arrange as desired atop Cream Cheese Spread.

VARIATION: Slice-and-bake prepared cookie dough may be substituted for the sugar cookie crust. Bake according to package directions.

The Cookie Basket

Cookie baskets make delightful gifts. A beautiful basket filled with an assortment of cookies makes an attractive and welcome addition to any table.

Alissa's Hawaiian Chocolate Chip Cookies

The original chocolate chip cookie, Toll House Cookie, got its name from a lovely old tollhouse owned by Mr. and Mrs. Wakefield of Massachusetts. Mrs. Wakefield first baked the original Toll House Cookies for guests at the Inn. Since then, there have been many variations, one of which is my granddaughter Alissa's favorite. She likes these cookies hot—right out of the oven!

In a large mixing bowl, cream butter or margarine with sugar until light and fluffy. Add eggs and vanilla extract; beat well. Combine flour, baking soda, and salt; mix well and gradually mix into creamed mixture. Stir in chocolate chips and nuts. Drop by rounded tablespoon onto ungreased baking sheets. Bake at 375°F for 9 to 11 minutes or until golden brown. Let stand 1 to 2 minutes; remove to wire racks to cool completely. Store in airtight container.

YIELD: ABOUT 5 DOZEN

1 cup butter or margarine, softened
¾ cup light brown sugar, packed
2 eggs, beaten
1 teaspoon vanilla extract
2¼ cups flour
1 teaspoon baking soda
1 teaspoon salt
2 cups (12 oz. package) semi-sweet chocolate chips
1 cup chopped macadamia nuts

Coconut Island Cookies

These cookies may take a little time to prepare but they are certainly worth the effort and go especially well with a cup of Kona coffee.

YIELD: ABOUT 3 DOZEN

½ cup butter or margarine, softened

1 cup brown sugar, packed

2 (1 oz. each) squares unsweetened chocolate, melted

¼ cup strong brewed coffee

1 egg, slightly beaten

2 cups flour

¼ teaspoon salt

½ teaspoon baking soda

½ cup sour milk

½ cup fresh or frozen grated coconut

ICING:

2 (1 oz. each) squares unsweetened chocolate

1 tablespoon butter or margarine

1 cup confectioner's sugar, sifted

2 tablespoons sour milk

⅓ cup fresh or frozen grated coconut

Cream together butter or margarine and brown sugar in small bowl until light and fluffy. Add melted chocolate, coffee and egg; beat well. Stir flour, salt and baking soda together. Add alternately to creamed mixture with sour milk, beginning and ending with flour mixture. Fold in grated coconut. Drop by teaspoonfuls onto baking sheet. Bake at 350°F for 10 to 12 minutes. Set aside.

TO PREPARE ICING: Melt chocolate and butter or margarine together. Add confectioner's sugar slowly with sour milk; mix until Icing is of spreading consistency. Spread about 1 teaspoon of Icing on each warm cookie and sprinkle with additional coconut.

Stephen's Giant Oatmeal Cookies

*M**y grandson, Stephen, enjoys munching on these Giant Oatmeal Cookies as his after-school snack or with ice cream for dessert.*

Beat together butter or shortening, both sugars, egg, water, and vanilla extract until creamy. Combine oats, flour, salt, and baking soda; stir into creamed mixture; mix well. Drop by rounded tablespoons onto nonstick or ungreased cookie sheet. Bake at 375°F for 12 to 15 minutes or until golden brown. Cool. Store in tightly covered container. Cookies will keep well for a few weeks.

YIELD: ABOUT 2½ DOZEN

1 cup butter or vegetable shortening, softened
1 cup brown sugar, packed
½ cup sugar
1 egg
¼ cup water
¾ teaspoon vanilla extract
3 cups oatmeal (quick or old-fashioned, uncooked)
1 cup flour
1 teaspoon salt
½ teaspoon baking soda

Special Desserts

The recipes in this section are perfect for those times when you're entertaining special guests. They're rich and attractive and will certainly impress the most discerning palate. But you don't have to wait for a get-together to try them out! Treat yourself to one of these decadent dishes any time of the week—your appetite will thank you!

Strawberry Mousse Dessert

soft and airy angel food cake paired with whipped cream, when set in a towering mold and turned out onto a polished dessert tray, this Strawberry Mousse Dessert makes a spectacular finale to any dinner.

Dissolve gelatin and salt in boiling water; add strawberries and stir until thawed. Chill until partially set. When partially set, whip until fluffy then fold in whipped cream. Place one-half of the cake pieces in bottom of 1½-quart mold or 8-inch spring from cake pan. Spoon one-half of the gelatin mixture over the cake pieces. Repeat process ending with two layers of cake pieces and two layers of the gelatin mixture. Chill in refrigerator until firm, about 2 hours. Unmold and garnish with additional whipped cream and fresh strawberries.

VARIATIONS: Lime, lemon or orange flavored gelatin may be substituted for strawberry. Pair flavored gelatin with fruits of choice.

YIELD: 8-10 SERVINGS

1 package (3 oz.) strawberry
   gelatin
Dash of salt
1½ cups boiling water
1 package (10 oz.) frozen
   strawberries
2 cups heavy cream, whipped
½ angel food cake, torn into 1
   to 2-inch pieces

GARNISHES:

Sweetened whipped cream
Fresh strawberries

Baked Hawai'i

A flambéed Baked Hawai'i (also known as Baked Alaska) can add a bit of "flair" to your dining table. This delicious dessert, often served at banquet or other formal affairs, will lends a wonderful sense of drama to the end of you meal.

Lay pineapple on side, cut off a horizontal slice one-third of the way down leaving crown intact. Hollow out center of pineapple leaving 1-inch wall; cut fruit into bite-size pieces and combine with pound cake then fill pineapple bowl. Top with ice cream and mold it slightly to conform to pineapple bowl. Place in freezer while preparing meringue.

To prepare the meringue, beat egg whites with salt in large, clean bowl until foamy. Add cream of tartar and continue beating until soft peaks form. Sprinkle sugar over the whites and beat on "high" until stiff and glossy. Cover ice cream in pineapple bowl with about 1-inch thickness of meringue, sealing it to the edge of the pineapple bowl; score surface, if desired. Place in freezer 30 minutes or until ice cream and meringue are firm but keep fruit from freezing. Place on baking sheet lined with parchment paper. Bake at 500°F for 3-4 minutes or until meringue is light brown. Flambé and serve immediately.

YIELD: 3-4 SERVINGS

1 medium pineapple with crown
2-3 slices pound cake, cut into bite-size pieces
1 pint ice cream, flavor of choice
Meringue (recipe follows)

MERINGUE:

4 egg whites at room temperature
Pinch of salt
¼ teaspoon cream of tartar
⅔ cup superfine sugar

VARIATIONS: Place a 3-inch round or rectangular piece of brownie, angel food cake or chiffon cake on foil-lined cookie sheet. Top with scoop of ice cream; freeze until very firm. Cover with meringue and proceed as directed above.

TIP: To flambé successfully: Choose a liquor with high alcohol content (80 proof or higher). Before browning the dessert, stick half of a washed eggshell into the meringue like a small cup. Just before serving, place ¼ cup liquor and a ladle in a small saucepan; heat the ladle and liquor just until liquor begins to bubble. Do not allow liquor to boil off, or it will not stay lit when you need it to. Ladle part of the liquor into the eggshell and ignite with a match. As the liquor burns, fill the warmed ladle half full with more warmed liquor and drizzle slowly into the eggshell, raising the ladle high as you can safely do. The flame will go out by itself when the alcohol burns off.

Liliko'i-Orange Cheesecake
Diamond Head Market & Grill

*K*evin Ro's Diamond Head Market & Grill generously shares its Liliko'i-Orange Cheesecake, one of the most popular desserts. The homegrown liliko'i gives flair to glazes and sauces for many island dishes. As a member of the Kapi'olani Community College faculty, Kevin actively supports the goals of its Culinary Arts programs by sharing his invaluable marketing knowledge and leadership skills with his students.

CRUMB CRUST: Combine melted better and graham cracker crumbs; mix well. Press mixture into greased parchment lined spring form pan. Press firmly up sides and onto bottom of pan. Refrigerate while filling is made.

CHEESECAKE FILLING: Place softened cream cheese in food processor, process until smooth and creamy (no lumps, scraping sides of bowl to incorporate any pieces of cream cheese). Add sugar, liliko'i concentrate, liliko'i liqueur, orange extract, orange zest, all-purpose flour, salt, whole eggs and egg yolks. Process or beat with mixer until thoroughly mixed; again, scrape sides of bowl. Pour batter into spring form pan. Bake at 350°F for 45 minutes. Check periodically to be sure top is not too dark; lower temperature to 325°F if necessary.

TOPPING: Combine sour cream, sugar and liliko'i concentrate; mix until well blended; spread over slightly cooled cheesecake. Return to oven. Bake at 375°F for 10 minutes.

COULIS: Combine liliko'i concentrate, sugar, water and corn syrup in saucepan; bring to boil. Combine water and cornstarch, make a slurry, and add to heated coulis mixture, stirring occasionally; return to a boil. Cool and chill in refrigerate until ready to serve with cheesecake.

Cool cheesecake and refrigerate. Before serving, spoon Liliko'i Coulis over top.

YIELD: 12 SERVINGS

CRUMB CRUST:

5 tablespoons unsalted butter, melted
2½ cups graham cracker crumbs

CHEESECAKE FILLING:

4 packages (8 oz. each) cream cheese, softened to room temperature
1¼ cups granulated sugar
¼ cup frozen liliko'i concentrate, thawed
2 tablespoons liliko'i liqueur (e.g., Alize), optional
1 teaspoon pure orange extract
2 teaspoons orange zest
¼ cup all-purpose flour
¼ teaspoon salt
3 eggs
1 egg yolk

TOPPING:

1½ cups sour cream
½ cup granulate sugar
2 tablespoons liliko'i concentrate

LILIKO'I COULIS:

1 can (12 fl. oz.) frozen liliko'i concentrate, thawed
¼ cup granulated sugar
¾ cup water
1 tablespoon light corn syrup
¼ cup water
2 tablespoons plus 2 teaspoons cornstarch

Lemon Verbena Crème Brûlée
Tangö Contemporary Café

*C*hef Goran Streng, co-owner of the popular Tangö Contemporary Café, shares his recipe for *Lemon Verbena Crème Brûlée, one of the more popular desserts at his restaurant. This dessert was popular at Monticello, Thomas Jefferson's home in Virginia, and received its name because of its caramelized sugar topping.*

YIELD: 6 SERVINGS

4 cups whipping cream
¾ cup sugar
Sprigs of lemon verbena or
    flavoring of choice
    (see variations)
1 egg
6 egg yolks

Place whipping cream, sugar and flavoring in a thick bottom saucepan over medium high heat. Bring to a boil, dissolving sugar. Turn off heat and let steep for 10 minutes.

Beat together egg and egg yolks in a medium bowl. Add the warm cream to the egg mixture, beating as you blend. Pour the mixture through a fine strainer into another bowl. Ladle mixture into individual ramekins or brûlée dishes. Place dishes in a pan and fill pan with hot water halfway up the sides of the dishes. Bake at 325°F for 25 minutes or until set. Cool in refrigerator. When ready to serve, sprinkle with sugar and "burn" with a blowtorch until golden brown.

VARIATIONS:
Kona coffee beans, macadamia nuts, bananas, fresh crushed ginger, coconut, rum or fresh fruits may be substituted for the lemon verbena. When using fresh fruits with high acidity, cook the fruits separately with sugar to draw out the acids; too much acid will keep the brûlée from setting.

Lime-Pineapple Refrigerator Cake

This light, airy cake is perfect for any occasion and wonderfully easy to make. Simply hollow out an angel food cake and fill it with lime-pineapple mousse.

Using a serrated knife, hold the knife horizontally and cut about ¾-inch off the top of the cake; set aside. Then hold the knife vertically to make a cut around the cake that is about 1-inch from the outside and center edges and about 1½ inches deep. Scoop out the center portion of the cake, being careful not to pierce through to the bottom. Place cake on platter; set aside. Save the scooped out cake crumbs for making other desserts.

TO MAKE THE FILLING: Drain syrup from can of crushed pineapple into a 2-cup measure; add enough water to make 1½ cups liquid; set pineapple aside. Bring pineapple-water mixture to boil in saucepan; add gelatin and salt; stir until gelatin dissolves completely. Refrigerate and chill until mixture begins to partially congeal; when partially set, whisk until fluffy. Fold in drained crushed pineapple and whipped cream.

Spoon Lime-Pineapple Filling into the hollow of the cake; replace the top of the cake and push down firmly. Spread top and sides of cake with sweetened whipped cream. Using a spatula, press nuts on to the sides of the cake, if desired. Arrange lime slices and pineapple on top.

TIP: Non-dairy whipped topping may be substituted for whipped cream.

YIELD: ABOUT 8-10 SERVINGS

1 angel food cake (bought or homemade)

FILLING:

1 can (6 oz.) crushed pineapple
1 package (3 oz.) lime flavored gelatin
Dash of salt
1 ¼ cups boiling water
2 cups heavy cream, stiffly whipped

TOPPING AND GARNISHES:

2 cups sweetened whipped cream
1 cup chopped mixed nuts, optional
Lime twists
Pineapple slices or chunks

Baked Apple Pancake

A kin to a Dutch Baby when baked, this classic German pancake puffs up incredibly, making for a very dramatic presentation on your breakfast table.

YIELD: 4-6 SERVINGS

2 tablespoons butter or margarine
2 large eggs
½ cup flour
½ cup milk
2 tablespoons brown sugar, packed
½ teaspoon ground cinnamon
Dash of nutmeg
1 Golden Delicious apple, peeled, cored and thinly sliced

Place butter in 10-inch cast iron skillet or 9-inch square baking pan and melt in oven while preheating (about 2 minutes).

To prepare batter, in medium bowl beat eggs slightly with wire whisk or hand beater; beat in flour and milk; set aside.

Sprinkle brown sugar, ground cinnamon and nutmeg over melted butter or margarine in skillet or pan. Arrange apple slices over sugar in skillet or pan; return skillet or pan to oven and bake until apples begin to soften and butter bubbles and begins to brown, about 5 to 6 minutes. Pour batter over apples. Bake at 400°F for 25 to 35 minutes or until puffed and brown. Immediately loosen edge of pancake and invert onto heatproof serving platter. Serve hot.

Quick 'N Easy Desserts

- Fill store-bought crepes with fruit, ice cream, pudding or sweetened whipped cream for a fast dessert.

- A new twist in dessert, fill ice cream cones with your favorite pudding or flavored yogurt.

- Mix pie filling with grated zest of lemon or orange, ground spices, lemon or lime juice, liqueurs or liquors and serve over ice cream, pudding, cake or brownies.

- Make an ice cream sandwich by putting two cookies or graham cookies (I love the chocolate ones—they are simply delicious) together with your favorite ice cream, flavored cream cheese, jam or frosting.

- Brush pound cake, angel food cake or butter cake slices with melted butter; roll in coconut or macadamia nuts and broil until light golden brown—drizzle with your favorite ice cream sauce.

- Use refrigerator cookie dough to make individual tarts.

- Give your cake a fancy look by placing a doily on the top and dusting with confectioner's sugar or cocoa. Remove doily.

Glossary

Abura-age – *Japanese name for deep fried tofu*

'Ahi – *Hawaiian name for yellowfin tuna*

Aku – *Hawaiian name for skipjack tuna*

Arare – *Japanese rice crackers*

Bahn trang – *rice paper wrapper*

Beni shoga – *pickled red ginger; condiment*

Cha gwa – *white cucumber*

Char siu – *Chinese sweet roasted pork*

Chinese five spice powder – *blend of star anise, cloves, fennel, peppercorns and cinnamon*

Chinese parsley – *cilantro*

Chow mein noodles – *Chinese soft-fried wheat or egg noodles*

Coconut milk – *juice from meat of coconut*

Daikon – *Japanese term for large white radish*

Dashi – *Japanese term for broth*

Dashi-no-moto – *Japanese instant powdered soup stock base*

Edamame – *soy beans*

Five spice powder – *blend of Chinese star anise, cloves, fennel, peppercorns and cinnamon*

Fish paste – *paste made from flesh of bonefish*

Furikake – *Japanese seasoned seaweed mix*

Gon lo mein – *Chinese noodle dish; usually stir-fried; may be baked*

Guava – *thin-skinned fruit with a sweet or slightly acid pulp*

Hapu'upu'u – *grouper (fish)*

Haupia – *Hawaiian coconut pudding*

Hawaiian red pepper – *small, hot, red chili pepper*

Hawaiian salt – *coarse sea salt*

Hoisin sauce – *Chinese soybean sauce used as a condiment or for flavoring*

Imitation crab – *crab–flavored fish product*

'Inamona – *roasted kukui nut, pounded and salted*

Inari sushi – *Japanese sushi rice in a cone–shaped abura-age*

Japanese vinegar – *rice vinegar*

Kaki mochi – *Japanese rice crackers*

Kālua – *Hawaiian method of cooking food in an underground pit called "imu"*

Galbi – *Korean barbecued shortribs*

Kew tao – *pickled scallions*

Kimchee – *peppery pickled vegetables*

Konbu – *seaweed, kelp*

Li hing powder – *Chinese powdered flavoring*

Liliko'i – *Hawaiian name for passion fruit*

Limu kohu – *Hawaiian name for a variety of seaweed*

Long rice – *translucent noodles made from mung beans*

Lū'au – *Hawaiian name for feast*

Lū'au leaves – *Hawaiian name for taro leaves*

Mahimahi – *Hawaiian term for dolfinfish*

Manju – *Japanese or Okinawan bean paste filled bun*

Mango – *gold and green tropical fruit*

Mirin – *sweet Japanese rice wine*

Mochi – *glutinous Japanese rice cakes*

Mochiko – *Japanese name for glutinous rice flour*

Moi – *Hawaiian name for small threadfin fish*

MSG – *monosodium glutamate*

Mui – *Chinese preserved fruit(s), usually plums*

Musubi – *rice ball*

Nam pla – *Asian fish sauce (Thai)*

Nam yue – *Chinese red bean curd sauce used for flavoring*

Namasu – *Japanese pickled vegetable dish*

Napa – *mild-flavored cabbage; a.k.a. won bok, makina or celery cabbage*

Nigiri Sushi – *Japanese sushi rice pressed into thumb shape and topped with seafood/omelet*

Nori – *Japanese name for dried purple seaweed sheets; laver*

Nori komi furikake – *Japanese seasoned seaweed mix*

Nori maki sushi – *vinegar flavored rice rolled in seaweed sheet*

Nuoc mam – *Asian fish sauce (Vietnamese)*

Oboro – *shrimp flakes*

Ogo – *seaweed*

Okazu-ya – *Delicatessens that sell Japanese take-out food*

Okinawan sweet potato – *purple sweet potato used by Okinawans and Filipinos*

Onaga – *Japanese term for red snapper*

Ono – *wahoo (fish)*

'Ono/'Onolicious – *meaning delicious*

Opah – *ocean moonfish*

'Ōpakapaka – *Pink snapper*

Oyster sauce – *Chinese oyster-flavored sauce*

Panko – *Japanese flour meal for breading*

Passion fruit – *yellow egg-shaped fruit with seedy pulp; a.k.a. liliko'i*

Poi – *Hawaiian staple; starchy paste made from mashed taro*

Poke – *Hawaiian seafood appetizer*

Ponzu – *mixture of sauce and citrus juice used as a dip*

Portuguese sausage – *garlic and pepper-flavored pork sausage; linguisa*

Pūlehu – *Hawaiian method of barbecuing meat*

Pūpū – *Hawaiian name for appetizer*

Rice stick noodles – *rice vermicelli*

Saimin noodles – *Japanese name for thin wheat or egg noodles*

Sake – *Japanese rice wine*

Sashimi – *very fresh raw fish*

Shibi – *Japanese name for yellow fin tuna; 'ahi*

Shiofuke konbu – *chopped, salted dried seaweed/kelp*

Shiratake – *Japanese gelatinous noodle-like strips made from tuberous root flour*

Shiso furikake – *beef steak plant flavored seasoning*

Sin geurng – *red ginger*

Soy sauce – *seasoning made from roasted corn and steamed soybeans mixed with malt – Mold, salt and water, then fermented.*

Sushi – *Japanese vinegar-flavored rice*

Sushi nori – *variety of nori used especially for sushi*

Taro – *tuberous root of taro plant; used to make poi*

Temaki sushi – *hand rolled sushi*

Tempura – *Japanese style fritters*

Teriyaki – *Japanese soy-flavored sauce*

Ti leaf – *broad green leaf of ti plant*

Tobiko – *Flying fish roe*

Tofu – *Japanese name for soybean curd*

Tortilla – *Mexican flat bread made of cornmeal or wheat flour*

Tsukemono – *Japanese style salted pickled vegetables*

Unagi – *Japanese name for eel*

Wasabi – *Japanese name for horseradish*

Yuzu – *Japanese citrus*

Weights & Measurements

TEASPOONS	TABLESPOONS	CUPS	OUNCES	MILLILITERS/ LITERS	PINTS/QUARTS
¼ tsp				1 ml	
½ tsp				2 ml	
¾ tsp	¼ tbs			4 ml	
1 tsp	⅓ tbs			5 ml	
3 tsp	1 tbs	1⁄16 cup	½ oz	15 ml	
6 tsp	2 tbs	⅛ cup	1 oz	30 ml	
			1½ oz	44 ml	
12 tsp	4 tbs	¼ cup	2 oz	60 ml	
16 tsp	5⅓ tbs	⅓ cup	2½ oz	75 ml	
18 tsp	6 tbs	⅜ cup	3 oz	90 ml	
24 tsp	8 tbs	½ cup	4 oz	125 ml	¼ pint
32 tsp	10⅔ tbs	⅔ cup	5 oz	150 ml	
36 tsp	12 tbs	¾ cup	6 oz	175 ml	
48 tsp	16 tbs	1 cup	8 oz	237 ml	½ pint
		1½ cups	12 oz	355 ml	
		2 cups	16 oz	473 ml	1 pint
		3 cups	24 oz	710 ml	1½ pints

Substitution of Ingredients

INGREDIENT	SUBSTITUTION
1 tablespoon flour (used as thickener)	½ tablespoon cornstarch, potato starch, rice starch, or arrowroot starch; or 1 tablespoon quick-cooking tapioca
1 cup sifted all-purpose flour	1 cup unsifted all-purpose flour minus 2 tablespoons
1 cup sifted cake flour	⅞ cup sifted all-purpose flour, or 1 cup minus 2 tablespoons sifted all-purpose flour
1 cup corn syrup	1 cup sugar plus ¼ cup liquid*
1 cup honey	1¼ cup sugar plus ¼ cup liquid*
1 ounce chocolate	3 tablespoons cocoa plus 1 tablespoon fat
1 cup butter	1 cup margarine, or ⅞ to 1 cup hydrogenated fat plus ½ teaspoon salt; or ⅞ cup lard plus ½ teaspoon salt
1 cup coffee cream (20 percent)	3 tablespoons butter plus about ⅞ cup milk
1 cup heavy cream (40 percent)	⅓ cup butter plus about ¾ cup milk
1 cup whole milk	1 cup reconstituted nonfat dry milk plus 2½ teaspoons butter or margarine; or ½ cup evaporated milk plus ½ cup water; or ¼ cup sifted dry whole milk powder plus ⅞ cup water
1 cup milk	3 tablespoons sifted regular nonfat dry milk plus 1 cup minus 1 tablespoon water; or ⅓ cup instant nonfat dry milk plus 1 cup minus 1 tablespoon water
1 cup buttermilk or sour milk	1 tablespoon vinegar or lemon juice plus enough sweet milk to make 1 cup (let stand 5 minutes); or 1¾ teaspooons cream of tartar plus 1 cup sweet milk
1 teaspoon baking powder	1/4 teaspoon baking soda plus ⅝ teaspoon cream of tartar; or ¼ teaspoon baking soda plus ½ cup fully soured milk or buttermilk; or ¼ teaspoon baking soda plus ½ tablespoon vinegar or lemon juice used with sweet milk to make ½ cup; or ¼ teaspoon baking soda plus ¼ to ½ cup molasses
1 tablespoon active dry yeast	1 package active dry yeast, or 1 compressed yeast cake
1 whole egg	2 egg yolks; or 3 tablespoons plus 1 teaspoon thawed frozen egg; or 2 tablespoons and 2 teaspoons dry whole egg powder plus an equal amount of water
1 egg yolk	3½ teaspoons thawed frozen egg yolk or 2 tablespoons dry egg yolk plus 2 teaspoons water
1 egg white	2 tablespoons thawed frozen egg white; or 2 teaspoons dry egg white plus 2 tablespooons water

Use whatever liquid is called for in the recipe.

Meat & Poultry Storage Time

MEAT	REFRIGERATOR (38°F TO 40°F)	FREEZER (0°F OR LOWER)
Beef (fresh)	2 to 4 days	6 to 12 months
Veal (fresh)	2 to 4 days	6 to 9 months
Pork (fresh)	2 to 4 days	3 to 6 months
Lamb (fresh)	2 to 4 days	6 to 9 months
Ground beef, veal, lamb	1 to 2 days	3 to 4 months
Ground pork	1 to 2 days	1 to 3 months
Variety meats	1 to 2 days	3 to 4 months
Luncheon meats	1 week	
Sausage, fresh pork	2 to 3 days	
Sausage, smoked	3 to 7 days	
Sausage, dry and semi-dry (unsliced)	2 to 3 weeks	
Frankfurters	4 to 5 days	2 weeks
Bacon	5 to 7 days	2 weeks
Smoked ham, whole	7 days	2 months
Smoked ham, slices	3 to 4 days	
Beef, corned	1 week	2 weeks
Left-over cooked meat	4 to 5 days	2 to 3 months
RAW POULTRY	**REFRIGERATOR (38°F TO 40°F)**	**FREEZER (0°F OR LOWER)**
Chicken and turkey		12 months
Duck, goose		6 months
Cooked poultry dishes		6 months
Fried Chicken		4 months
FROZEN COMBINATION FOODS	**REFRIGERATOR (38°F TO 40°F)**	**FREEZER (0°F OR LOWER)**
Meat pies, cooked		3 months
Swiss steak, cooked		3 months
Stews, cooked		3 to 4 months
Prepared meat dinners		2 to 6 months

Index

Oven Pot Roast, 119

Oxtail Stew, 31

oyster sauce, 139, 193

P

pancetta, 141

Pan-Fried Teriyaki Salmon, 130

panko, 129, 193

Pansit, 143

passion fruit, 161, 192-193

Pasta Casserole, 142

peanut, 4, 67, 113

peas, 70, 101

pecans, 57, 155

pineapple, 13, 22, 63, 68, 81, 109, 183, 189

poi, 23, 193

popcorn, 4, 15, 75

pork, 13-14, 17-18, 22, 26, 31, 44, 50, 55, 68, 77, 96, 108-110, 118, 141, 143, 192-193

Pork country-style ribs, 108

Pork loin back ribs, 108

pork ribs, 109

Portuguese Sausage, 14, 193

Portuguese Sweet Bread, 1, 5-6, 156

pot roast, 119

potato, 5, 33, 70, 91, 193

prawns, 65

pretzels, 91

Prune Frosting, 160

Prune Mui, 8, 10, 85

prunes, 8-10, 85, 160

R

raisins, 70, 88, 134, 162, 173

ramen, 17-18

raspberries, 147, 150, 174

Red Coconut Candy, 15

rice noodles, 67, 138, 143

rice vermicelli, 138, 193

Roast Beef, 17, 31, 115

Roast Pork with Rosemary, 110

Roasted Lemon Soy Chicken, 120

Roesti Potatoes, 43-44

rosemary, 110, 116, 119

round steak, 21

S

saimin, 1, 17-18, 21, 193

sake, 25, 37, 101, 193

salmon steaks, 130

Salty Preserved Prunes, 10

Sashimi Salad, 67

Saucy Ribs, 108

Savory Pretzels, 91

sea bass, 56, 67, 103

Sesame Chicken Orientale, 58

sesame seeds, 17-18, 21, 26, 58, 67, 97, 99, 101, 104, 113, 118, 139

Shabu Shabu Nabe (*Japanese-Style One Pot Dish*), 112

shallots, 49, 56, 58, 60, 72-73, 116, 137

shellfish, 133

shibi, 32, 193

Shibi No Tataki (*Blackened Tuna*), 32

shiofuke konbu, 100, 193

shiitake mushrooms, 112

shiofuke konbu, 100, 193

shirataki, 193

shiso furikake, 15, 193

short ribs, 116, 118

shrimp, 2, 17-18, 31, 41, 59, 65, 100, 103, 126, 133, 137-138, 143, 193

Shrimp Tempura, 17, 59, 126

sin geurng, 67, 193

Snowballs, 57

Spaghetti with Bolognese Sauce, 107, 141

SPAM®, 19, 26, 50, 202

SPAM® Temaki Sushi, 19

spareribs, 108-109

Spicy Oriental Corn Chips, 84

Spicy Seasoned Hawaiian Salt, 80

spinach, 56

Stacked Apple "Pies", 173

Star Fruit Seed, 9

Stephen's Giant Oatmeal Cookies, 179

stew meat, 117

stewing beef, 23

strawberry, 165, 181

Strawberry Mousse Dessert, 181

About Muriel Miura

Muriel Miura is a best-selling author of local cookbooks. Muriel graduated from the University of Hawai'i's home economics program and earned her graduate degrees in home economics education from the University of Hawai'i–Mānoa and Columbia University of New York City.

Muriel may be most recognized for her nationally televised cooking shows from the 1970s: *Cook Japanese Hawaiian Style* and *The New World of Cooking with Muriel*. Comfortable with all types of cuisines, Muriel is known to add a personal touch of Hawai'i to her foods.

Muriel has written more than twenty cookbooks, including recent ones such as *Japanese Cooking–Hawai'i Style*, *Hawai'i Cooks with Spam*®, *Hawai'i's Party Food*, *What Hawai'i Likes to Eat*™, *Homemade Gifts of Sweets and Treats*, *Cookies from Hawai'i's Kitchen* and *Hawai'i Cooks and Saves*.

A Honolulu-born kama'āina, Muriel lives with her husband in Honolulu and spends a part of the year with her daughter and her family on the Mainland. She is also involved with a number of community service projects in her spare time since her retirement from The Gas Company.

About Galyn Wong

*I*n 1990, Galyn Wong joined Mutual Publishing as Director of Special Sales and Projects which included the research and development of Mutual Publishing's cookbooks. *What Hawai'i Likes to Eat™: Hana Hou* is her official debut as an editor although she has managed numerous other culinary projects including recipe searches, creating ideas for editorial photography and managing the food photo shoot.

Galyn started her culinary career on the service side working in numerous restaurants including New Tokyo Restaurant on Beachwalk, The Willows and Kyoya. She quickly moved on to become Banquet Matre'd at the Sheraton Waikīkī. Her love of food also led her to the other side of the table as she became a connoisseur of island cuisine by frequently dining at Honolulu's diverse mix of restaurants and familiarizing herself with food preparation and tastes.

A passionate animal lover, she spends her time off with her much-loved part-Samoyed buddies, Kolohe and Bear, at the waters' edge near Tongg's surf spot as well as learning how to train and raise cockatiels. She is also an avid practitioner of healthy homemade food for pets.

Notes

Notes

Notes